THE
SCOTTISH COMPANION

edited by Rhoda Spence

A BEDSIDE BOOK
OF DELIGHTS

EDINBURGH

RICHARD PATERSON

Richard Paterson Limited, Edinburgh

first published 1955

Printed in Great Britain by
Robert Cunningham and Sons Ltd.
Alva

CONTENTS

ACKNOWLEDGEMENTS

THE editor and publishers wish to thank all those who have helped in the preparation and production of this book.

Acknowledgements are due for permission to include copyright quotations as follows:

Margaret Leigh: *Highland Homespun* (Phoenix House); Helen B. Cruickshank: 'In any Glen' from *Sea-Buckthorn* (H. T. Macpherson); Margaret Winifrede Simpson: 'Moray Waters' from *Aisles of Song* (Moray Press); Tom Longstaff: *This My Voyage* (John Murray); Andrew Young: 'Mountain View' from *Collected Poems* (Jonathan Cape); W. H. Murray: *Mountaineering in Scotland* (J. M. Dent and Sons); F. Marian McNeill: *The Scots Kitchen* (Blackie and Son); Alastair M. Dunnett: *The Highlands and Islands of Scotland* (by permission of The Brewers' Society); Edwin Muir: 'Childhood' from *Collected Poems* (Faber and Faber); Robert Rendall: 'Orkney' from *Country Sonnets and Other Poems*; J. B. Salmond: 'Kate Kennedy—Her Day, A St. Andrews Bardic Ode' from *The Old Stalker and Other Verses*; George Campbell Hay: 'Kintyre' from *Wind on Loch Fyne* (Oliver and Boyd).

Acknowledgements are also due as follows for permission to reproduce photographs facing the pages noted:

A. D. S. Macpherson, page 4; J. Allan Cash, pages 5 and 41; The Scottish Tourist Board, (top) page 14; *The Scotsman*, (bottom) page 14; Robert M. Adam, page 15; *Country Life* and David G. Crichton, Esq. (owner of the portrait), page 40; Tom Weir, pages 52 and 53; The National Portrait Gallery of Scotland, page 64; Messrs Thomas Agnew and Sons (publishers of the large engraving), page 65; A. J. B. Strachan, by courtesy of The National Trust for Scotland, page 106; G. M. Cowie, page 112; The National Museum of Antiquities of Scotland, page 113; Sir Ian Forbes Leith, Bart. (owner of the portrait), page 122; Anthony Murray, Esq. (owner of the portrait), page 123.

The illustrations are by William McLaren and John Mackay.

Introduction

Most people have a pile of books congenial to the hours between waking and sleeping, a grown-up substitute for the toy of childhood, and often as familiar from long perusal. An anthology of verse, a favourite classic, a book of essays, the selection reveals the mind of the reader at a glance. For 'Bedside books are the heart's testament', as a Scottish poet once wrote, describing how an apparently stolid business man betrayed the romantic within him by keeping a volume of Blynd Hary's *Wallace* for night reading. The choice and size of the pile varies from adolescence to old age. In the teens, when late reading is frowned on, and there never seems to be enough time to devour all the books which open up the fascinating world of literature, the bedside table (and sometimes the bed as well) is weighted down with old and new discoveries. In later life the choice narrows to perhaps half a dozen volumes, winnowed over the years, along with the most recent biography or travel odyssey.

What qualities must a new bedside book possess to merit admission to the pile? It would be a bold editor who would lay down rules, but possibly the most obvious requirement is that the contents should be sufficiently intriguing to keep the reader awake, but not brutally harrowing or depressing. A personal belief of the writer is that the articles should lead the imagination down unfrequented byways, and be written with such obvious pleasure that the reader shares the contributor's experience in an intimate fashion.

But, more difficult still to define, what should a new Scottish bedside book contain, following as it does innumerable miscellanies laden with the choicest treasures of the centuries? The answer would seem to be fresh material, and the assistance of contemporary Scottish writers and illustrators treating subjects especially congenial to them. That we have been fortunate in obtaining these things the contents list will show. Our contributors have entered warmly into the spirit of the book and are ready to lead the reader down the mysterious loanings, into the ballad-haunted valleys and through the remote mountain-lands of Scotland, or to hold the scrying-glass to those curious vestiges of history which bring the past to vivid life.

With each feature there are quotations for dipping into, extracts in prose and poetry intended to suit the mood of the article they accompany. The effort here has been to avoid the hackneyed, and to reveal fresh vistas in the territory explored. So, if the section on *Glamourie* lacks such eminently suitable ballads as 'Tam Lin' or 'The Wife of Usher's Well', it is because these are already richly familiar to the lover of otherwhere, while the inclusion of the lesser-known 'Mermaid' ballad and of 'Harmisay', the last poem from the pen of Lewis Spence, gives the authentic *frisson* or pleasurable 'grue' and enlarges the horizons of Scottish weirdrie by another bow-shot into the land of Elfame.

How receptive is the mind at bed-time, ready for 'the cinema of day-dream' which is in the ante-room to sleep! Was there ever a country so full of material for its scenarios, so crowded with subtle characters, so rare in the wild beauty of its landscape as ancient Alba, the source of our themes, which we hope will in turn be the source of your pleasure.

R.S.

Edinburgh, *August* 1955.

vi

OFF IN THE CAR

by *Neil M. Gunn*

We never felt the year was complete unless we made one trip round the north-western Highlands. Three days would do it in a car from Inverness and when it was over, well, we had been there, seen once again the mountains we knew so well, the long lochs and the lochans, the moors and the inlets of the sea. It might have been a prescribed treatment to keep body and mind right; anyway, unless we had it, a feeling of deficiency haunted us in an odd way.

Perhaps there are vitamins that cannot be done up in a bottle, not even by a magician, much less by the family chemist. Nor is that so fantastic as it may seem, because after all a certain kind of wizardry can project on to a screen pictures of the desirable places. Surely that should be at least a tolerable substitute? On the contrary, it can be worse than nothing if it reminds us of the trip we failed to take.

For of course there is far more to it than seeing Suilven plain or Ben More Assynt in a cloud, the battlements of Ben Loyal against a remote sky or Ben Stack overhead. Though from Torridon northwards, what individualists the mountains are, not only in shape but in character, with, at times, in certain lights, an uncanny suggestion of something more!

However, I must not be lured by the light so soon, the light that is never twice the same, for a lot of practical things have to be done first, like packing the car. The wonderful thing about a well-packed car is not just the neatness that finds the rear part sufficient but the certainty that when you arrive everything will be there. I am not even trusted by my wife to lift in a suitcase. My job is to see to the car, so I make the most of it. Over the years this division of labour has become so defined

1

that it is not even mentioned. The primus stove has always been there, and the car has never failed to bring us home. And if this sounds like perfection, at least the memory of it is perfect anyhow. For were the primus missing, it would be a poor-fisted man who could not make a fire and even wonder, as the primeval scent of old heather roots and withered bits of trees assailed his nostrils, why he bothered with fancy contraptions anyhow. But let me qualify that rash statement at once lest it be overheard by those whom we so instinctively placate by touching wood. I am even prepared to formulate a law: *Do your best to have everything right, so that when it goes wrong it will go better.*

If I were unexpectedly asked what were the most memorable parts of the trips, the camping sites would jump to my mind. Though camping is hardly the word, for after one or two experiences of a small canvas tent, particularly during one moist windless night when midges in black battalions did their combined best with a preference for eyelids, we left canvas and the too solid damp earth alone. We slept in our car, but we got it specially arranged for this purpose. It was a simple arrangement, too, and consisted in reversing the back seat (back to front), then sliding forward the two front seats and folding their backs over towards the back seat until one level was attained throughout. It was so easy to do that I hadn't to do it. My job on arrival was to find water, fill the kettle, get the fire going and do the cooking. Long before I was finished she would stroll over to see how I was getting on. I have even in my time been complimented on the way I have dealt with trout in a frying pan, for the capacity of a freshly caught trout to twist and curl up so that only one inch of it is being cooked at a time is very remarkable—almost as remarkable as the pleasure a woman gets from watching a man doing what is normally her job.

But around all the ongoings is the place we have arrived at, the known place, the birds, the scents of heather and bog myrtle, the rather rare wild flower still in the same spot, the feel of moss in the fingers, the headland or the lochan with the reeds or the water lilies, the mountain or the immense stretch of moor, the arch of a small bridge, the arch of the sky. And if you don't exert the right pressure at the right spots the trout will be either cooked in bits or broken in bits. The important

2

thing is that at last there is no need to hurry. You have arrived.

I think even the voice takes on a slightly different intonation, but that may be the effect of the stillness, the silence, upon the listening ear. This silence comes around the frying pan as it crackles merrily. The right amount of salt is very important and you can lean the plates towards the heat. The chances are that by this time she is so taken with everything that the loaf gets sliced and small containers and implements laid out in a sort of dream-like way. Out of the wonder of it all comes: 'What a good smell!'

Smell first, and then taste. Hunger. Water running under the tongue. The old well hasn't run dry. Far from it. It is more inexhaustible than the frying pan. Munching—just plain munching—and looking around, and pausing to look at something that looks back. How good plain bread is, if you idly chew it until it melts and slips away, leaving its flavour behind! Supposing you take a bite of plain bread, by itself, that is, and not with a whole strawberry dexterously removed from the jam. Though it is good then, too. Once in a remote place we had tea with a young man who first placed butter from his cow on a bannock, then crowdie softened with cream from the same cow, and then topped the two layers with home-made black currant jam. Always prepared to try anything once, I found my jaws working plenteously amid a richness that melted in so surprising a harmony that I would have laughed at the wonder of it if I could.

The meal over we prepare for our evening stroll. On such tours we believe in having a method, for it's about the only thing you can break and still have. If there are hills at hand we set off to climb one, not missing much in the way of wild life, and even being lured from the hill by a whistle or cry we are not too sure of. In the early summer months the wind generally dies down in the evening and the atmosphere is very clean. The half-light can be magical in the primitive sense, not 'poetic' but alert as the ears of an invisible hare, especially if you are round at the back of the place you hadn't been going to, and haven't been there before. Now you know what ears and eyes are for; or at least they tell you in a new way, especially when the ears begin listening for the silence beyond silence. You hold your breath then.

So in one way or another we wander around until the twilight loses its queer glimmer, and in the deepening dusk we return to the car, seeing it from a little distance in a familiar and unfamiliar aspect as if it were transfixed in a strange dream of its own. A man can develop an odd affection for a car, particularly if he has shared its faults. A woman can just develop an affection for it.

The inside is all one double bed with a quilt on top and pyjamas on the pillows. This is not my work. It's high life with sleep on cushioned springs and a ledge to hold a glass by my left hand. I fetch fresh water in the kettle, for there is nothing like a kettle's spout for making sure that too much water doesn't get into the glass when the time comes. My wife has a ledge on her right hand. The responsibility for providing the kind of drink that best sustains individual life and liking is entirely mine. There is a time for all things and this is the time of times, when we lie back and look out through the windows as the darkness deepens like a lingering benediction that presently lets sleep fall.

The odd thing about sleep now is that one can awake very early, perhaps at four in the morning, and feel fresh and alert; then, like an animal, close one's eyes and go off again. We have had some rare glimpses of moor birds and waders as they whistle and flit in this grey dawn that is a second twilight. You really are in their world and see them in an objective impersonal way that is curiously strange and delightful. But perhaps this is the kind of vision that brings you back.

However *the* hour for one at least is the full awakening followed by breakfast. I may say that anticipation is so keen that I am all but forcibly ejected into my duties, though as I get out I hear—and am deliberately intended to hear—how luxury in full possession can swathe itself in more than a sigh or even a deep gurgling chuckle. But I don't mind. In fact I enjoy pottering around in a mindless way, and if it is the kind of fresh sunny morning that draws the eyes afar and bare feet land on a flat thistle in the grass any natural comment by me does no more than add an audible refinement to the luxury I left behind. I boil the kettle and I boil the eggs and in due course return with a tray. She regards me with the kind of expression that a lady in a very expensive hotel assumes, after she has first used her

The timeless spirit of the North-West bespells such landscapes
as this, where the road leads to the cool silence of the hills

Water, woodland, and rocky heights, gloriously arranged, make
a faery-land forlorn by the shores of Loch Maree

bedside telephone, been given the waiter, explained exactly what she wishes for breakfast, and the waiter appears.

Two more points about a car as a bed: midges rarely, if ever, come in through the side ventilators, and if they do they fasten on to the surrounding glass instead of the human face; if there is wind, park the nose of the car in its eye—result, no draughts.

Then we pack up and go on to our next resting place; though we have one or two sites where we have stayed for over a week on end.

In all of them there have been memorable nights, and before a winter fire they can send the mind wandering. For treasure of this kind is not like money in a bank, in that however the account is drawn on it never gets less. Indeed it seems to get richer, for though it may be taxed by memory, memory is both bank and banker, and promptly adds the tax to the capital. In terms more appropriate for an amateur cook, you eat your cake and have it.

There are two or three loops which we encompass, with remarkable connecting sea roads when time is no matter. For a simple round trip one could hardly do better than start from Inverness, fork right at Achnasheen, take it easy going down Glen Docherty, meander along Loch Maree, climb up to drop down through gorgeous pines to the sands of Gairloch, then up and on by Poolewe and Gruinard (with its wonderful site) and so back by Dundonnell.

But any attempt at itineraries would be merely a run of evocative names; and even then how could one add up in any kind of arithmetic all that lies, say, between Ullapool and Laxford Bridge, by way of Achiltibuie, Lochinver, the coast road to Kylesku, the ferry, and on to Scourie? All I'll say is that we go slowly and the going itself is wonderfully good.

Yet I have not mentioned the loop that will be remembered when the others are not forgotten. We go there as we might go home. From Lairg, by Loch Shin, to Loch More and Laxford Bridge, then north to the wide sands of Balnakill Bay, before packing again after we have got soaked with sea and light. The Pentland road, with forks for Altnaharra, and—but let me finish in the wilds of Caithness not far from the Sutherland border. In a certain spot, which shall be nameless, we have stopped longer than at any other. Red deer are there, and

5

mountain hares and a stream. I have talked about frying fresh trout, but I should despair of attempting to describe how to fry four salmon cutlets when the flakes are so fresh that they break away from the curd. Even if you burn your finger in an anxious moment and stick your finger in your mouth, you merely get the flavour beforehand. For there has always been something truly blessed about that place.

WHAT'S YOUR HURRY?

If you want a job of work done in the West, and ask a man whether he can get it finished by a certain time, he raises his eyebrows and says in a slow, soft voice 'What's your hurry?' He may go on to explain that tomorrow he must attend a neighbour's funeral, and the next day, if the weather is good, he must give Sandy a hand with his peats or go fishing with Angus; but more often he will put that searching and unanswerable question, 'What's your hurry?' For after all, what *is* your hurry? If it is a pair of boots you want to have soled you can always wear the old pair with holes, or if it is too wet for that, sit by the fire and dream until the cobbler is ready. Provided that there is food in the cupboard . . . we can afford to wait, and the other fellow's delays will only give us a good excuse for doing nothing ourselves. The author of the Book of Genesis clearly regarded work as a curse. Now I am so far bitten with the Sassenach bug of industry that I am inclined to think work a blessing, but measured, leisurely work, except where you are circumventing the weather, as when you rush in a load of hay: but then the element of sport enters into it, which makes all the difference. It is hurry that is the curse. All frenzied activity— all hustling and bustling, scurrying and hurrying, buzzing and jazzing, hooting and tooting, are destructive of peace and beauty, and will in the end degrade rational humanity into a collection of jigging automata in a mechanical world.

Margaret Leigh: *Highland Homespun*

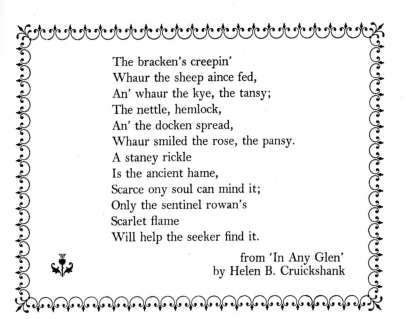

The bracken's creepin'
Whaur the sheep aince fed,
An' whaur the kye, the tansy;
The nettle, hemlock,
An' the docken spread,
Whaur smiled the rose, the pansy.
A staney rickle
Is the ancient hame,
Scarce ony soul can mind it;
Only the sentinel rowan's
Scarlet flame
Will help the seeker find it.

from 'In Any Glen'
by Helen B. Cruickshank

I saw the stems of fir and larch, straight as pillars, some dark in shadow, some fired to red by slanting sunbeams, and through the stems a glimpse of loch, blue as the fabled Mediterranean seen through olive groves; and beyond that the bronze and purple of distant hills, and above the hills, clear sky and slow billowing clouds. The very stillness of the air gave much to hear, since nearer sounds were more subdued, and distant ones had wider range . . . the alarm note of birds, so frequent when I first came into the wood, had ceased, and a few dry days had silenced the smaller burns. I could hear the click-clock of a fisherman's oars as he rowed out to the haddock bank, and the chut! chut! of a blowing porpoise. In the township across the water women were talking and calling their hens. Farther away someone was pulling down a boat with a harsh grinding of pebbles. Half-way across the loch a mottled flotilla of eider-ducks were mingling their quacking noises with a liquid crooning note, which sounded like a polite but scandalised person saying softly 'Oh no! Oh no!' On the hill a shepherd called his dogs.

Margaret Leigh: *Highland Homespun*

A portion of the High Street facing St. Giles Church was called the *Luckenbooths*, and the appellation was shared with a middle row of buildings which once burdened the street at that spot. The name is supposed to have been conferred on the shops in that situation as being *close shops* to distinguish them from the open booths which then lined our great street on both sides; *lucken* signifying closed. This would seem to imply a certain superiority in the ancient merchants of the Luckenbooths; and it is somewhat remarkable that amidst all the changes of the Old Town there is still in this limited locality an unusual proportion of mercers and clothiers of old standing and reputed substantiality.

. . . The central row of buildings—the *Luckenbooths* proper—was not wholly taken away till 1817. The narrow passage left between it and the church will ever be memorable to all who knew Edinburgh in those days, on account of the strange scene of traffic which it presented—each recess, angle, and coign of vantage in the wall of the church being occupied by little shops, of the nature of Bryce's, devoted to the sale of gloves, toys, lollipops, &c. These were the *Krames*, so famous at Edinburgh firesides. Singular places of business they assuredly were; often not presenting more space than a good church pew, yet supporting by their commerce respectable citizenly families from which would occasionally come men of some consequence in society.

Robert Chambers: *Traditions of Edinburgh*

As befitted trinkets given as love or betrothal tokens, the Luckenbooth Brooches sometimes bore charmingly sentimental mottoes or the initials of the lovers concerned. 'Wrong not the heart whose joy thou art', one motto besought; 'Let me and thee most happy be', ran another of the inscriptions. 'My heart ye have and thir I creve' and 'I fancie non but the alon' were amorous approaches which must surely have touched the most hard-hearted lassie.

8

THE LUCKENBOOTH BROOCH

by Ian Finlay

NEITHER stick nor stone of the Luckenbooths survives, but until about a century and a half ago much of the life and some of the best business of the capital went on around those odd and possibly rather ramshackle buildings in the High Street of Edinburgh. The name applied to the buildings directly opposite

St. Giles' Kirk, and also to a row of buildings in the middle of the street. *Lucken* probably signifies locked; so that, as Chambers long ago explained, the Luckenbooths seem to have been closed shops as distinct from the common, open booths which lined both sides of the ancient street. 'This', he went on, 'would seem to imply a certain superiority in the merchants of the

Luckenbooths; and it is somewhat remarkable that, amidst all the changes of the Old Town, there is still, in this limited locality, an unusual proportion of mercers and clothiers of old standing and reputed substantiality.'

If nothing of the booths themselves survives, their name is a commonplace in all the antique shops of Scotland. A tradition persists that the little heart-shaped brooches which must once have been so numerous were first made and sold there. It may well have some basis in fact. Jewellers were almost certainly among those merchants of 'reputed substantiality' who plied their trades in those tiny shops, some no more than a few feet deep. The brooches are not valuable trinkets, even in these days of bloated and ridiculous prices, but in their simplicity and unpretentious charm they are attractive.

The basic form is a plain outline of a heart, as often as not with a curl or twist to the point. Usually such a brooch is surmounted by a crown. As with so much else in Scotland, there is a link here with Scandinavia, where the heart brooch was a common token, and no doubt the original models were brought in to Leith and other east coast ports. Frequently there are twin hearts interlinked, and the simple outline is elaborated with loops and chevrons and spikes. The pin, on all early examples, is just a small, flattened bodkin swivelling on one arm of the heart and brought up short on the other. At once suspect any Luckenbooth brooch which is fitted with a spring pin behind! Later brooches are often set with garnets and such semi-precious stones, and the silver which is the usual material is occasionally, with very small brooches, replaced by gold, although I have only met with two or three of the more precious metal. The silver itself is frequently not of very good quality, and it is most likely that quantities of the brooches were even made in base metal, although naturally most of these have been thrown away and lost.

It is probable that the majority of the little ornaments were cast in moulds and then worked up by hand, finished by a bit of engraving, or were cut out of sheet metal largely to stock patterns. Jewellers must have turned them out as a routine task, for often the technique is crude; but here and there a maker's hall-mark will be found, or even a town mark. Do not, however, dismiss a brooch without hall-mark as of 'dud' metal,

for goldsmiths did not normally trouble to stamp objects so tiny —too tiny indeed to accommodate the marks! The smiths were often perfunctory enough in stamping teaspoons, many times the weight and bulk of the brooches, since the quantity of silver is relatively small. By no means all the brooches were made in the vicinity of the Luckenbooths, for actual brooches and records show that the far north produced a good deal of jewellery of this kind. One type, indeed, seems to be limited to Inverness.

The use to which most of these brooches were put is fairly obvious. The heart, and more particularly the twin hearts conjoined, symbolically surmounted by a crown, points to a token of betrothal, and if anything were wanted to confirm this the initials generally inscribed on the backs of the brooches would do so—the initials of donor and recipient, and now and then also the date of the gift and, one assumes, the troth. In addition there may be some inscription indicating that the recipient possesses the donor's heart and longs to have hers in exchange. The considerable quantities of Luckenbooth brooches surviving demonstrate that the custom of giving such tokens must have been widespread, even among the humblest. Some such tokens may have come into use before the end of the seventeenth century; they were certainly common throughout the second half of the eighteenth and far into the nineteenth—in fact, probably long

B

after the Luckenbooths themselves were swept away. There are tales that the brooches were used in some country places as luck tokens or charms against the evil eye and witchcraft. A fairly late account states that such brooches were pinned by mothers among the clothes on the left leg to ward off harm from their babies.

It is no longer so easy to pick up Luckenbooth brooches in shops or salerooms, for a keen market has made them eagerly sought after. Some of the private collections, too, have found their way into museums instead of dispersing into circulation again as they would probably have done in another age. Collectors must be wary of modern imitations, although most of those are so crude and obviously commercial that anyone whose eye has become accustomed to the real thing would not look twice at them. In the unexplored corners of the country—and Scotland still has numbers of remote country houses which come into this category, happily—there must be many a fine little brooch lying with other trinkets in a drawer never opened. Here and there among them there may even be a real prize: some medieval precursor of the Luckenbooth, a simple hoop or octagon of tarnished silver inscribed obscurely in base Latin.

These small brooches, like their medieval predecessors, were also believed to be endowed with the property of protecting children from witchcraft. The Reverend James Hall describes how they were used at the close of the eighteenth century. 'They always fix it to girls somewhere on the left hip and on boys about the middle of the left thigh.' The same writer remarks that he once met an old woman who had worn a brooch fixed on her clothes upon the left hip for more than fifty years to preserve her from mischief. Mothers when nursing, frequently wore them to prevent the witches from taking away the milk and to keep off evil from infants.

IN THE MARGIN OF MORAY

by Elizabeth Macpherson

You see our farm the moment you leave the little moorland station and turn your eyes to the hills and the south. Behold us then, very small and grey, clinging with all our sprawling grasp to the skirt of the Knock of Moray. Our fields are the very last visible before the dark waste of Dava Moor swallows all the prospect. Dava with its peaty bogs and more than a hundred little lochs hidden in its secret breast is the boundary between Morayshire and the highlands proper.

We love the place where we live but are not quite so prejudiced by its wild free air and spaciousness as not to realize that to the eye of the outsider our situation appears more precarious than æsthetic. The truth is that the Knock of Moray is a lumpish hill lacking grandeur and the encompassing moor depends entirely on the play of strong sun and racing spring wind to lend it animation.

As one laboriously climbs the steep road leading to the south there is an undoubted dreichness in the scene. It is difficult, too, to believe that the highway with its swerves and braes and narrow bridges is the main road to the city and the south. That it closely follows the old wild way by which the reiving Highlanders made their forays into the fat lands of the Laich of Moray is much more credible until a succession of heavy lorries with trailers reeling behind them come skidding and swerving past the terrified pedestrian to reassure him that it is still twentieth century Britain and that traffic congestion is as much a problem in Dava as in Glasgow. As the last great trailer load of housing components on its way to the housing schemes of Forres shrieks down the hill, the traveller draws a long breath and turns back to look on the way he has come. Quite the best place to do this is at the entrance to our farm. Looking back how different and jubilate the prospect now!

The country falls in swift yet gentle steps or terraces down through the plumy woods of Altyre and Darnaway, down to the sleepy fertile fields of the Laich, down to the shores of that narrow shining firth whose farther horizon is filled with the blue enchanted mountains of Ross and Sutherland.

The Laich of Moray is a curious place to find behind the cold shoulder of the north-east of Scotland. It enjoys a climate best described as balmy and should you sound incredulous it sleepily indicates its roses flowering all the year round. It never ceases to surprise me, when we make our weekly journey from our hilly fastness every week to market in Forres, to find emerald green fields full of red and white cows grazing placidly there whilst at home our own cattle are snugly penned in byre and fold and wait for the humans to give them their meals of silage and straw. Blizzards rage about the granite outcrops we call arable land here while down on the flat of Moray the tractors are ploughing beneath clouds of birds plumaged in sunlight.

No wonder the medieval church with its genius for finding settings for its religious houses should have chosen Moray to be a lantern in the north and should have built there abbeys and priories, colleges and churches, and even a great cathedral. Sometimes I think this sense of ancientness gives Forres its untroubled outlook. After all if prelates, priests and kings wandered through time, here in this place, one cannot help taking the historic outlook. This serenity allows her to ignore problems of the mushroom present. No doubt the business man wanting on market day to hurry through the town finds her attitude to traffic less chaotic than fantastic, but after all why should he want to hurry through Forres? Why indeed? There is no other place in Scotland more comfortable to do nothing in than Forres.

Part of the charm of Morayshire is that it contains such contrasts in so narrow a space. A bare twenty miles separate Forres from Grantown but a mere measure of distance is no indication of the gulf which lies between the two towns. Forres dreams of milk and honey and opens a dreamy eye upon a flowery scene. Grantown is all romance and temperament and looks for eagles' feathers under the summits of the Cairngorms. But as you are

The face of Moray offers contrasts between the smiling harvest-
fields of its straths and the colder uplands fringed by Dava Moor

High summer in the woods of Morayshire yields exquisite glimpses like this study from the Knockando–Dallas road

still standing at our farm gate you are ten miles yet from Grantown, and as far, too, from Forres, since we are as near midway as makes no odds. The road to Grantown continues to rise steeply even after you leave us. It will rise till it reaches the little hill station of Dava and then will descend to find Grantown hiding behind a railway bridge and a castled crag. But you are not nearly there yet.

A mile after you leave us you see that the Knock of Moray at last lies behind you and no longer makes a hugger-mugger of the prospect. Once round its last obtrusive bump you find yourself looking on a scene of romantic grandeur. The immediate country is moorland proper with great unfenced solitudes of coarse grass and loch. Here and there are big stacks of black peat cut by the shepherds and gamekeepers who are the sole human inhabitants of all this spaciousness. Since this is sheep country there are none of the wide arable fields which are the characteristic of cattle lands. Little green spaces are hacked out of the sides of rolling hills, and ruined cottages tell the story of people who found the way of life here too arduous and left. Through the middle of the moor flows the River Dorback. It is on its tempestuous way to meet the Divie far down the country. Both rivers then will join the Findhorn, that most erratic of Scottish rivers, whose past history of floods and devastation gave us one of the classics of our literature, *The Moray Floods* by Dick Lauder.

In the clear upland atmosphere the distant Cairngorms assume an astonishing airy splendour. They are all snowy summit and gashed and tragic corrie. At their feet lies the valley of the upper Spey and another country from the one you now travel.

I always think the best season to enjoy the Dava is the spring. It is true the wind is still thin, but by the middle of March the song of a myriad larks above the vanishing snow wreaths of bitter winter is something never forgotten. However cold the wind, the rapturous affirmation of the larks singing as if it were the first world ever born, and their song the newest minted therein, is enough to make you forget every doubt that ever cankered the human heart. This is a miracle and this is true. Nor are larks the only denizens of that wild free air. Plovers wheel and call, curlews solitary amongst the echoing hills make solitude exquisite, and black-headed gulls screaming in the sedges of invisible lochs affirm the mystery. Grantown is a seemly little town to come on after all this. Its main street sweeps about in lawns and avenues and almost overwhelms the little Adam-designed orphanage standing shyly aside.

But we'd be less than human if the view that interested us most at this time were not the one which we see from the scullery window which shows us a trim line of pylons crossing a neighbour's field. When that line of pylons is completed we shall be within measurable distance of having electricity. I have lived here for seventeen years, and that, I think you will admit, is a fair time in which to find out all about an apprenticeship to paraffin. Paraffin had been the motive fuel here till bottled gas came along to make us feel quite sophisticated and slick. But bottled gas did not by any means do away with lamps for lighting nor oil heaters for cold corridors. I am on intimate terms too with *reeky peters* which you light for going to do the byres on dark winter mornings and nights. My knowledge of pressure lanterns for the deep litter house is as near exhaustive as can be, whilst paraffin stoves of all kinds are as familiar as A.B.C. but a lot smellier. When electricity comes we feel we'll have no more to ask for.

Electricity is the ultimate amenity. Or are we naïve in thinking so? The next time we need a tractorman, will his wife look carelessly at the modernized cottage we offer complete with all other mod cons in addition to electricity and say 'It's a nice hoosie but it's terrible far awa' '? 'Terrible far awa' ' means there are no neighbours near, and a general lack of human bustle and throng. Most folk find loneliness far harder to thole than the lack of conveniences. Better a slum in the town with a crowd than a modern house in the country with a hill for neighbour. I sometimes wonder if we ourselves and the rest of the folk hereabouts are not the queer ones. We find a rich and satisfying life each within the stone boundaries of our upland fields. Each scattered farm is a little world complete with humans, fields and beasts all integrated with the changing seasons of the rounding year. Because of our aloof lives each circumstance that touches us takes on personality. Fields get names, implements assume a sex and the beasts of course are considered as individuals. No one finds this fanciful and it is as a matter of course that when we sell a cow to a neighbour the first question he asks is 'What

16

is her name?' Folk who have no knowledge or understanding of the beasts of the field miss much, for in them we can see with humility a great many of our own qualities. Like us they can be bullies, greedy and inquisitive. Like us again they can be gentle, loving and faithful. Like us, too, they are creatures of an hour and share our brief mortality. The dust of the fields in which we labour is the beginning and end for both of us, so we are the more inclined to walk humbly with our God, which is as happy and seemly a way to live our mortal lives as one can want.

In salubrity of climate, Moray is not inferior to any, and in richness and fertility of soil it much exceeds our other northern provinces. The air is so temperate, that when all around is bound up in the rigour of winter, there are neither lasting snows nor such frosts as damage fruits or trees. . . . Corn the earth pours forth in wonderful and never-failing abundance. Fruits of all sorts, herbs, flowers, pulse are in the greatest plenty, and all early. While harvest has scarcely begun in surrounding districts, there all is ripe and cut down, and carried into open barnyards, as is the custom of the country; and in comparison with other districts, winter is hardly felt. The earth is almost always open, the sea navigable, and the roads never stopped. So much of the soil is occupied by crops of corn, however, that pasture is scarce; for this whole district is devoted to corn and tillage. But pasture is found at no great distance, and is abundant in the upland country, and a few miles inland; and thither the oxen are sent to graze in summer when the labour of the season is over. Nowhere is there better meat nor cheaper corn, not from scarcity of money but from the abundance of the soil.

Sir Robert Gordon of Straloch, 1640

DUNPHAIL IN THE MORAY FLOODS

The meal-mill and the carding-mill of Dunphail on the right bank of the Dorback were utterly destroyed by the flood, and the miller and his family were only rescued with the greatest difficulty and after superhuman efforts by the neighbours. Says the miller:

'Every moment we expected the crazed walls of the house to yield, and to bury us in their ruins, or that we and it together should be swept away. We began to prepare ourselves for the fate that seemed to await us. I thank Almighty God that supported me in that hour of trial. I felt calm and collected, and my assistant was no less so. My little brother, too, said 'he was na feared''; but the woman and the lad were frantic, and did nothing but shriek and wring their hands. While we were in this situation, we suddenly saw about sixty people coming down the bank, and our hopes revived. . . . All our attention was fixed on their motions. They drove a post into the ground, and threw the end of a thick rope across to me. This we fixed to a strong beam, and jammed it within the front window, whilst they on the bank made fast the other end of it to the post. A smaller rope was thrown over. This I fastened round the boy's waist, and he was dragged through the water to the bank, supporting himself all the way on the larger rope that was stretched between the window and the post. The lass lost her hold, and was taken out half-drowned; but, thank Providence! we were all saved.'

Sir Thomas Dick Lauder: *An Account of the Great Floods of August* 1829 *in the Province of Moray and Adjoining Districts*

18

MORAY WATERS

Where Moray's lilting waters run
My love be with them every one,
Where Moray's waters flow serene
Singing of peace their banks between!

Laugh, April, their green ways along!
September, swell thy golden song!
No lovelier rapture shalt thou know
Than there where Moray's waters flow!

My wish be with you every one,
In winter's snow or summer's sun
Heart of delight and dream's desire
O singing streams of Morayshire!

from *Aisles of Song* by Margaret Winifrede Simpson

20

IN THE SCOTS GLAMOURIE

by Lewis Spence

Iᴛ is the enchantment, the veritable magic of her environment, which has made Scotland the most poignantly mysterious and haunting region in Europe. Nature is and always has been her supremest artist, exercising a powerful sorcery of soil and atmosphere the influence of which surpasses the achievements of that human genius which seeks to imitate it. There lies in Scottish air a secret virtue which, instead of encouraging or provoking the artist to creation reveals to him the secret magics of a process already accomplished, granting him the overwhelming vision of that which has long been completed, which ridicules his puny efforts and triumphantly laughs them to scorn. Why seek to paint a scene whose arcane colours cannot be seized, why make verses upon that which is already poetry come to sight, why seek to awaken melody where the mightiest of musics continually resounds? When you approach the very cauldron in which the elements of art broil and seethe you feel that to prepare the moulds for the same is a business more for gods than for men.

Scotland is indeed a laboratory of those strange and inconceivable forces which underlie all the processes of art and emotion. In certain of its fastnesses we behold the most primitive landscapes of the early world where creative chaos appears to have been frozen or petrified in the midst of some wild upheaval. You are caught up in the primal immensities, you are in a region of phantasmagoria, of the sources of divine energy, you realize that this is a matrix of legend whence arise the vapours of tradition. These roll from the cauldrons of the hills down upon the plains, where they assume the fantastic shapes of myth.

It was in one of these regions of overflow, rich with the

21

coloured phantasms which fall from the hills and vibrant with the echoes of legend, that I became conscious of what it signifies to inherit in some degree the seership of these mysteries. The height above the sea, once a place of refuge and rendezvous for fugitive Jacobites, gave back upon the Plain of Angus, a broad expanse of faerie fields, forming a green apron to the Sidlaws, whose very name enshrines a tradition of elfin, one of the richest among the minor provinces of legend in Scotland. The brownie's castle, the tumuli of Vikings slain in battle with the Picts, the deep dens concealing ancient mills which had to be protected by charms lest the fairies should split the great stones which ground the oats, became vignettes in a personal book of tradition unforgettable. The soil seemed indeed the gospel-page of an individual religion as sacred as it was secret, far more profoundly fanatical indeed than ever was conceived by dervish, saint or eremite.

This plateau, on summer mornings, was a place of cock-crow and the high call of peacocks from the great house over the way and as I lay in my cot hearkening to the challenge of the militant birds to others far off, a thin chain of trumpet-sound receding into distance, I came to realize the magic of the remote, the first fantastic fact in the code of Faerie. And if I clambered up to the attic windows of the nursery and gazed from them past the pied fields of Fife toward the great grey lapse of the Tay firth it was to behold goblin craft swimming the weaving waters, phantom carvels bearing harpers and pipers who brought home cargoes of songs from Levantine gardens.

And as the doctrine of enchantment unfolded and found the food it sought in books, the affairs of everyday receded and grew more and evermore unsubstantial. School became an intolerable purgatory, games merely a mitigation of educational boredom. *The Secret Commonwealth* of Kirk was, of course, a revelation, a testament, Dalyell a godsend, the *Letters on Demonology* a banquet, the ballads the hymnology of my creed, Robert Chambers's *Popular Rhymes* a bedside book of hours.

In time I came to realize that the countryside was not the only reservoir of the mysterious power which had taken such complete possession of me. As I discovered, many of the little towns of Scotland overflowed with this goblinesque influence. Such spots as Thrums, Anstruther, Blairgowrie, Cupar Angus,

Falkland and the like were drenched with it, these crow-stepped gables appeared as stairways to some aeriel enclave of our native magic. At Roslin and Earlston there were fainter emanations. In other areas which I will not be so cruel as to mention the influence had been abraded by tripper visitation. In our greater cities I have found nothing of it at all.

In the Western Isles, of course, the tradition of this peculiar witchery has been preserved in a literature of extraordinary value and distinction. Not a little of it, as is self-evident, is of early Irish origin. Whence came those tales in Lowland phrase which tell of *The Red Etin, Childe Roland, The Well at the Warld's End, Rashiecoat* and the rest of that enchanted series? The first and third are assuredly Hibernian and were, in all likelihood, carried to the Scottish Court by those Highland sennachies who so frequently found their way eastward in the days of the earlier Stewarts, while the second is as clearly Arthurian in its coil and craft, yet strongly coloured by native skill and predilection, especially in its depicture of the fairy realm. Its description of elfin interiors is believed by some to enshrine memories of Elgin Cathedral, that flame-wasted prodigy of medieval afflatus. *Rashiecoat* is, of course, a Scots recension of the theme of *Cinderella*, which has circled the earth and has been recorded in more than three hundred variants.

But more than one of our Lowland Scots poems of note reveal the deepest impress of glamorous influence from a native die. Such, I feel, is the comic extravaganza entitled 'King Berdok', preserved in the Bannatyne MS, which recounts how Berdok, King of Babylon, grew fain of Mayiola the gowk or cuckoo of Maryland. When he first saw her she was milking her mother's kye, an Arcadian touch. He put her into a creel and carried her off, but on reaching home found nothing in the basket but an owl's nest. Bent on capturing the maid, he returned to her dwelling, at which her father, the King of Faerie, levied war upon him. The god Mercury came to his aid, however, and transformed him into a bracken bush. Here 'Maryland' is merely a late corruption of the expression 'Middel-erd', an old Scots name for Fairyland. The thing is woven of mist and sunbeams, its scarcely definite shapes put in with a silver needle threaded with thistledown.

Nor who, perusing the 'Dreme' of the monk Lichtoun, surely

an illuminatus of the Scots Mysteries, can question that it had its source in the caverns of our weirdrie? Lichtoun was an earlier Scots Coleridge and his 'Dreme' recalls the background of the Lake poet's 'Kubla Khan'. Languishing in prison, he frees himself by a gymnastic magical gesture and drifts in spirit across the lands of earth, after which he sails to Paradise in an enchanted ship. Here he finds the Patriarchs roasting strawberries at a fire of snow. Subsequently he is lost in a fog for seven years and at last penetrates to a mystic reach where white whales disport themselves on the greenest of meadows.

The ballads, however, are the most vital projections of the Scottish sense of Otherwhere. The old stupid Radical theory that they 'arose out of the consciousness of the people' is perhaps the most grossly absurd which has ever insulted critical opinion. Indeed it may be said in a word that scarcely a line of inspired imaginative verse in the entire gamut of Scots literary invention originated in the democratic consciousness. The ballads are rigidly aristocratic in spirit and sentiment and were clearly the production of a caste of highly skilled literary craftsmen, the protegées of a proud and consciously superior nobility. Certain circumstances in this matchless body of verse yield the impression that its makers, if they did not actually draw their technique and inspiration from the same sources as did the official Highland bards, had at least adapted, or inherited the 'rules and cautils' known to their Celtic colleagues or predecessors. What are known as 'runs' in Celtic poetry, that is 'set pieces' kept in stock for the description of familiar incidents, appear to have their doublets in the Lowland ballads of the older type in those stock verses which recur from time to time in certain passages, more especially in such refrains as 'a wan water', 'he's mounted on his berry-brown steed', 'he ta'en her by the milk-white hand', and all those expressions which recur like the refrains of a litany.

And it is notable that the heroes of these intensely precious productions, among the brightest jewels of human fantasy, are persons of mystical name and origin, so utterly mysterious indeed that their identity quite escapes the most vigorous investigation: Lammikin, Glasgerion, Jellon Graham, Foodrage, Hinde Etin, Bearwell, Leesome Brand, and a host of others. These names strike a weird note in the mind as might the words of a forgotten tongue uttered in the depths of a cavern. What in the name of Mystery herself were these beings whose indecipherable titles seem the echoes of primeval sounds? 'Hinde', as a term, is usually bestowed upon supernaturals, its common reading implies a demon, as in 'the Hinde Knight', used of the Devil, while 'Etin' is merely the Old English word for 'giant'. Jellon, the sinister and blood-stained, has been construed as 'Julian' by editors. Lammikin, the thwarted mason who slew Lord Wearie's wife and child, because his lordship would not discharge his debt for building his castle, was, despite his name (a gentle diminutive) a sanguinary monster. Doubtless the story which tells of his crime had its origin in the antic belief that no great building might be raised unless it be mortared with the blood of an innocent victim. The name 'Glasgerion' has a Kymric fall. He was a harper and a king's son and he slew 'the lither lad' who betrayed him with a princess. These are the names of shadows from a region of shadows lying on the far side of a river across whose sable waters none can see.

At times in reading or pondering on these immortal fragments from the world's weirdest literature we are never quite certain whether we walk on good Scots earth or tread the shores of Phlegethon. The Wife of Usher's Well, a sorceress, lost her three sons at sea. One eerie night their wraiths returned to her wearing hats made of the birk, the headgear of supernaturals, and ate and drank as though in life. Early belief recognized no difference between body and soul and the dead were thought of as living an existence of their own in their graves and as eating and drinking there. We are, in the land of balladry, groping in a demesne of half-light where we encounter 'littel men' walking 'between a water and a wa' ' who prophesy to us, a land of haze and grammarye, where nothing is beheld with perfect vision. This is indeed the lapse of the Celtic Underworld, the land of the Sidhe, as is revealed by the descriptions of the clothing and horse-furniture of its inhabitants, the ancient deities of our Celtic forefathers. It must follow that the makers of our ballads were the heirs of the Celtic bards and their poetry the broken reflection of that remote glory which rivals the victorious miracle of Hellenic epos.

The writhing figures of the merciless women of the flood appear in this riotous mythic tapestry much as they do on the walls of Mar's Wark, in ancient Snawdoun, that miraculous ballad in stone. The demon-woman with the fish's body will not be denied her prey.

> Her een were of the skyie blue,
> Her lips did mock the wine.

Words of marvel fallen from veridical poetic lips! However æsthetically attractive, she had, like her sister the siren, a homicidal streak, and woe worth the hero who fell in with her:

> Aboon the stream his wraith was seen,
> Warlocks tirl'd lang at gloamin'.

Phoebus! What a line! And what a language for artists to work in! It beggars the resources of the world's linguistic treasuries and it lies outcast at our own back doors. The verse holds the echoes of a mysterious drum beating at sunset across a dread water.

When another mermaid bound a cloth about the brow of Clerk Colvill to ease a megrim, he called aloud in agony. As he perished, the diabolical sea-dame swam off, well pleased with her morning's work. Still more vindictive was that mermaiden of Angus, who, on being cheated of her prey, screamed after the young laird who had been rescued from her clutches by the wit of his henchman:

> 'Lorntie, Lorntie,
>   Were it na your man,
> I had gart your heart's bluid
>   Skirl in my pan.'

Most doomful of all, 'The Demon Lover'. This matchless, unapproachable act of genius flashes upon the sense stark as a landscape fletched with lightning, the chiefest miracle in the gallery of Scots enchantment, a glimpse of the infernal unparalleled.

> She hadna sailed a league, a league,
>   A league but barely three,
> Till grim, grim grew his countenance
>   And gurly grew the sea.
>
> He strack the top-mast wi' his hand,
>   The fore-mast wi' his knee;
> And he brake that gallant ship in twain,
>   And sank her in the sea.

Shrouded in ghostly music by Scotland's greatest composer as 'Ship o' the Fiend', it has found a second greatness. In casting the runes of melody in this shape magical Hamish MacCunn riveted his name for ever to the most supreme achievement of Scottish traditional poetry.

If our ballads are more eloquent of the mysteries of Other-where, our legends nearly approach them in glamorous effectiveness. They have created shapes the most strangely unique in popular lore—the brownie, the *uruisk*, the *banshee*, the washer-at-the-ford, all varieties or derivatives of the fay. Among the most fearsome is that sister or type of the *banshee* known as Meg Mollach, who was attached to the ancient family of Tulloch-gorum in Strathspey and locally known as 'Hairy Meg'. She served at table and it was said that whatever dishes were asked for appeared as though floating on air, lighting on the board quite safely. Meg had, however, a widespread reputation for uncanny powers throughout the Central Highlands and cats were sometimes sacrificed in the dreadful rite of *taighairm* so that she might come to their rescue and bargain for their lives with their tormentors, to whom she gave some magical secret in return for their freedom.

The *glaistig* was the spirit of a woman who had once belonged to a family, a kind of ancestral ghost. At times she conferred the gift of second sight upon her favourites. More dreadful and repellent was the *bean-nighe*, or washer-wife, who washed the shrouds of the dead by night. If caught while exercising this funereal occupation she could be compelled to predict her captor's fate. Demonic in intent were the *sluagh*, or bands of the dead who flew through the air by night to slay sheep and cattle and even to injure mankind, though to be able to do so they had first to capture a living man and compel him to shoot their fatal arrows at the object of their spleen. These are but a few of the uncanny shapes which remain in folklore as memorials of the vast army of the inhabitants of Scotland's demesne of Other-where.

The catalogue of the Scottish mysteries is a long one indeed and I have set it forth elsewhere. The important matter is bound up with the question: whence came the profoundly arcane inspiration which created this extraordinary complex of thauma-turgical tradition? Foreign influence may be appealed to, even

C

so, it is self-evident that whatever the airts whence it drifted, its general aspect and complexion were bestowed upon it by the indwelling genius of our land, which possesses the secret of magically transforming whatever it may receive into its own unique shapes and symbols.

O dinna ye spy yon castel braw
　　Ayont the gress-green riggs o sea?
There's a tower intill't and a bower intill't
　　And a louping lyon has power intill't,
Rampin' amang the winds that thraw
　　Yon banner bousteouslie.
O whaten a castel is yon, ma minnie,
　　That harles the hert's bluid oot o me
And beckons me owre a warld o watters
　　To seek its weird or dee?

Yon castel braw, ma bonny bit hinny,
　　It is the Scottis Glamourie;
There's a spell intil't and a well intil't
　　And the sang o a siller bell intil't,
But the braes abune it are dowf and whinny,
　　And the bracken buries the lea.
It's noo a ship wi' the haar for sail,
　　And syne a strength, as ye may see,
Forbye it's a hill wi' a hollow ha',
　　Whaur the fludes sough eerilie.

THE MERMAID

. To yon fause stream that, near the sea
   Hides many ane elf and plum   *[deep hole]*
And rives with fearful din the stanes
   A witless knicht did come.

The day shines clear—far in he's gane,
   Where shells are silver bright;
Fishes war loupin' all aroun',
   And sparklin' to the light.

When, as he laved, sounds came sae sweet
 Frae ilka rock and tree,
The brief was out, 'twas him it doom'd
 The mermaid's face to see.

Frae 'neath a rock, sune, sune she rose
 And stately on she swam,
Stopp'd in the midst, and beck'd and sang
 To him to stretch his han'.

Gowden glist the yellow links
 That round her neck she'd twine;
Her een were of the skyie blue,
 Her lips did mock the wine.

The smile upon her bonnie cheek
 Was sweeter than the bee;
Her voice excell'd the birdie's song
 Upon the birchen tree.

Sae couthie, couthie did she look,
 And meikle had she fleech'd;
Out shot his hand—alas! alas!
 Fast in the swirl he screech'd.

The mermaid leuch, her brief was gane
 And kelpie's blast was blawin',
Full low she dook'd, ne'er raise again,
 For deep, deep was the fawin'.

Aboon the stream his wraith was seen
 Warlocks tirl'd lang at gloamin';
That e'en was coarse, the blast blew hoarse,
 E'er lang the waves were foamin'.

*Recovered from the recitation of a lady who
heard it sung by the servants in her father's
family about 1758*

It was deemed highly imprudent to speak of the fairies, when about to
        pass the places which they were supposed to haunt.

This superstition continues to prevail, though one would suppose it must now be antiquated. It is only a year or two since
an itinerant puppet-showman . . . brought a complaint of a
singular nature before the author as Sheriff of Selkirkshire.
The singular dexterity with which the show-man had exhibited
the machinery of his little stage, had upon a Selkirk fair day
excited the eager curiosity of some mechanics of Galashiels.
These men, from no worse motive that could be discovered
than a thirst after knowledge beyond their sphere, committed
a burglary upon the barn in which the puppets had been consigned to repose, and carried them off in a nook of their plaids,
when returning from Selkirk to their own village.

      'But with the morning cool reflection came.'

The party found however that they could not make Punch dance,
and that the whole troop were equally intractable; they had
also, perhaps, some apprehensions of the Rhadamanth of the
district, and, willing to be quit of their booty, they left the puppets seated in a grove by the side of the Ettrick, where they
were sure to be touched by the first beams of the rising sun.
Here a shepherd, who was on foot with sunrise, to pen his
master's sheep in a field of turnips, to his utter astonishment
saw this train, profusely gay, sitting in the little grotto. His
examination proceeded thus:

    Sheriff. You saw these gay-looking things? What did you
      think they were?

    Shepherd. Ou, I am no that free to say what I might think
      they were.

    Sheriff. Come, lad, I must have a direct answer.

    Shepherd. Ou, sir, troth I am no that free to say that I mind
      wha I might think they were.

    Sheriff. Come, come sir! I ask you distinctly, did you think
      they were the fairies you saw?

    Shepherd. Indeed sir, and I winna say but I might think it
      was the Good Neighbours.

Thus unwillingly was he brought to allude to the irritable
and captious inhabitants of fairyland.

                        Sir Walter Scott in a note to *The Monastery*

John Stuart, being interrogated anent the crime of witchcraft, declared that upon Wednesday, the third day of January instant, Bessie Weir in Pollok town came to the declarant late at night, who, being without doors near to his own house, the said Bessie Weir did intimate to him that there was a meeting to be at his house the next day; and that the Devil, under the shape of a black man, Margaret Jackson, Margery Craige, and the said Bessie Weir, were to be present. And that Bessie Weir required the declarant to be there, which he promised; and that the next night, after the declarant had gone to bed, the black man came in and called the declarant quietly by his name; upon which he rose from his bed and put on his clothes, and lighted a candle. Declares that Margaret Jackson, Bessie Weir, and Margery Craige did enter in at a window in the gavel of the declarant's house, and that the first thing that the black man required was that the declarant should renounce his baptism, and deliver himself wholly to him; which the declarant did, by putting one hand on the crown of his head, and the other on the sole of his foot. . . . Declares that thereafter the Devil required all their consents for the making of the effigies of clay for the taking away the life of Sir George Maxwell of Pollok, to revenge the taking the declarant's mother, Janet Mathie. Declares . . . that they wrought the clay; and that the black man did make the figure of the head, and face, and two arms to the said effigies. Declares that the Devil set three pins in the same —one in each side and one in the breast—and that the declarant did hold the candle to them all the time the picture was making; and that he observed one of the black man's feet to be cloven; and that his apparel was black; and that he had a bluish band and handcuffs, and that he had hoggers on his legs without shoes; and that the black man's voice was hough and goustie.

Witch Trial held at Paisley Feb. 15, 1677
Touching the Bewitching of Sir George
Maxwell

HARMISAY

The muir is mirk, yet no wi' nicht,
　The muir is bricht, but no wi' day,
But be it nicht or be it licht
　Is nocht to the fouk o Harmisay.

For theirs is a dowfer nicht than nicht,
　An' theirs is a glintler day than day;
They hae the glaik that glamours the sicht,
　The fouk o the clachan o Harmisay.

A skelp on a stane wi' a watten rug
　An' the onding swirls atowre the swarth,
A whusher i' the corbie's lug
　An' the carlin's weird sweels roond the airth.

I saw the lowe o the Sabbat fire
　Aneath the mune on Harmisay,
The mingle o a scarlet gyre
　Wi' glints o siller glawnicy.

Wi' scudderin haste the roe ran by,
　The wildroun hare raced owre the lea,
By-ordnar sicht nae mair had I—
　Ye get but glisks at Harmisay!

Lewis Spence

'WILL YE NO COME BACK AGAIN?'

by *Winifred Duke*

ALL his life Prince Charles Edward enjoyed mysteries, subter-
fuges, and concealments. He loved to lurk behind an alias, and
frequently hid his real identity under an assumed name. When
early in 1744 he left Rome secretly for Paris he styled himself
Don Biaggio of the Spanish court. After the disaster of Dunkirk
he loitered in and around Gravelines, where he was known as
Monsieur Douglas. On the voyage to Scotland in 1745 he wore
the dress and personality of a French abbé, while even during
his wanderings amidst the Western Isles, in addition to becom-
ing Betty Burke, he and his quarter-master-general O'Sullivan
adopted the name of Sinclair, and pretended to be father and
son. From his earliest days Charles was enmeshed in a web of
intrigue, backstairs interviews, secrecy, cyphers, pass-words,
and disguises, so that dissimulation became second nature to
him. Something of the schoolboy was contained in his make-up,
as it was in that of Sir Walter Scott, who derived immense
satisfaction from the complications which arose out of his denial
that he wrote *Waverley*, and the myriad speculations as to who
did.

After the collapse of the 'Forty-five and its tragic reper-
cussions the Prince's movements on the Continent were open
enough for a time. Following his arrest and banishment from
Paris, however, in December 1748 he went to Avignon, from
whence, as Voltaire says, 'he hid himself from the whole world'.
No doubt he delighted in mystifying everyone, the remaining
adherents of his own party, the French king and ministers, the
courts of Europe, their emissaries and spies, with startling

rumours of his whereabouts, and sensational speculations as to his movements. He was reported as being in innumerable places at one and the same time. Postboys were alleged to have recognized him driving through Lyons to Metz. Other people maintained that they saw him in Poland or Sweden, and again boldly entering the French capital. There was even a whisper that he was dead. In May of 1749 he made a short stay at Venice, and the following year he was in Paris 'under the habit of a Capuchine Fryar', a disguise he certainly assumed at times. Other measures he took to disguise his identity were pitting his face to counterfeit smallpox, pretending to be a lackey, wearing a beard or false nose, and darkening his eyebrows. 'One of my intelligencers', writes the British Ambassador, Sir Horace Mann, in January 1753, 'went so far as to say that he saw him in the streets the 4th instant, but so disguised as to make it extremely difficult to know him, having painted his face with red and coloured his eyebrows with the deepest black . . . that he followed him and saw him go into the Scots College.'

During August of 1750 another rumour touching him arose, this being of serious illness. In reality the Prince, never enjoying better health in his life, was preparing for a great hazard, no less than a secret visit to England. Charles was on the eve of an expedition even more crazy and less likely to succeed than his impetuous and unheralded descent on Scotland five years earlier. As in the first instance, Scotland received no warning of his coming. That he intended to go is revealed in a memorandum written in his own hand. 'My full powers and commission of Regency renewed, when I went to England in 1750, and nothing to be said at Rome, for every thing there is known.' Further jottings reveal briefly dates and places. 'Parted ye 2d. Sep. Arrived to A. (Antwerp) ye 6th. Parted from thence ye 12th. Sep. E. (England) ye 14th, and at L. (London) ye 16th. Parted from L. ye 22nd, and arrived at P. (Paris) ye 24th.'

What was Charles's object in running such a risk? It was considerable, as the price of thirty thousand pounds was still on his head, and at any moment he might have been recognized and betrayed. Sundry anecdotes are told of his secret and mysterious stay in the capital. Dr King, of St. Mary's Hall, Oxford, relates that the Prince partook of tea with him, and afterwards his servant remarked on the visitor's likeness to certain busts of

Prince Charles on sale in Red Lion Street. Lady Primrose, widow of an executed loyalist, also received an unauthorized call from him, an unexpected honour which startled and discomposed her considerably. It was rumoured that he went for a day to Oxfordshire and interviewed supporters of his party there.

One wonders whether, as he slunk about the hot, stinking streets of the city he had thought to enter as conqueror five years before, he may have caught a glimpse, from his place of concealment amongst the ignorant and hurrying crowds, of his hated rival who defeated him at Culloden, the Duke of Cumberland. 'The Butcher' had somewhat regained the popularity which had waned not long after the 'Forty-five, and his was a familiar, loudly-acclaimed figure to the populace. Did Charles, probably muffled in a cloak, stand to watch him ride past, cheered by the mob, bitter memories of that terrible April morning rending his heart? During his hurried and surface glimpse of England he must have realized how any feeling for the exiled house and the broken Cause was non-existent. He made no attempt to reach or get in touch with Scotland, but wandered round the Tower, examining the possibilities of blowing up one of the gates, and presided over a meeting of about fifty Jacobites in a room off Pall Mall. He is said to have declared that if he could raise a force of four thousand men he would put himself at their head. Nothing came of the visit, and Charles returned to the Continent, once more to disappear from the world's gaze. Politically he was ceasing, nay, had ceased to be of any importance or menace, but he kept up his existence of mystery and concealment, drifting from dingy inn to sordid lodging, in low water financially, perpetually intriguing, plotting, suffering repeated disappointments, yet never losing hope.

It was during his brief stay in London that Charles renounced the Romish faith and was received into the Anglican communion 'in the New Church in the Strand'. Another note of his verifies this. 'To mention my religion of the Church of England as by law established, as I have declared myself when in London the year 1750.' The change of creed gave him no advantage, beyond gaining him the lukewarm approval of a few remaining adherents, and causing the deepest grief and chagrin to his father and brother at Rome. He was five years too late. As Carlyle of

Inveresk says, such a step, if taken at Edinburgh, would have secured him the low-country commons.

In February 1752 the Prince was at Ghent, styling himself the Chevalier William Johnson. He was borrowing from any who would lend him money, and preparations for what came to be known as 'the Elibank Plot' were maturing steadily. Lochgarry and Dr Archibald Cameron met him at Menin about the end of September, and he disclosed his plans to them. General Keith, at the head of Swedish troops, was to land in the north of Scotland. Until he did so Charles did not wish the Scots to rise. He himself was so certain of success that he expected shortly to be in London, and avowed 'that he was determin'd to give the present Government no quiet untill he succeeded or dyed in the attempt'. The plan was for the persons of the Royal family to be seized, and Charles proclaimed king. The scheme miscarried, its eventual result being the arrest and subsequent execution of Dr Cameron, the last Jacobite martyr, but much mystery and uncertainty prevail as to whether at the time of 'the great affair of L.' (London) Charles was actually again on English soil.

Some authorities confuse this supposed second visit with his first one. Lady Primrose is reputed to have sheltered him, while different accounts refer vaguely to his being 'on the coast' during the crucial time. There is (or was) an old house situated near Godalming, long declared to be haunted by the ghost of Prince Charles Edward. In the late autumn of 1752 a certain Madame de Mézières, General Oglethorpe's sister, and a fanatical Jacobite, crossed from France and took up residence there for a while. It is not wholly improbable that the Prince was her guest, and, afraid of being seen by daylight, paced the grounds at night, thus giving rise to the story that his ghost was afterwards seen. It was a time of suspense and uncertainty for him, a dreadful hazard at stake, this hourly awaiting news from London that the blow had been struck and he might at any moment be escorted in triumph to the capital. Instead, he suffered another harrowing disappointment, and once more stole away to his ignoble life of skulking and concealment. George II was, according to one authority, aware that the Prince had ventured himself on English soil, but when consulted as to what measures should be taken replied that nothing was necessary.

When Charles was tired he would return to the Continent again, which is precisely what occurred.

Yet Jacobitism was not wholly dead. During a seven weeks' strike of Northumbrian keelmen in 1750, some of these actually proclaimed Charles III from a stile in Elswick fields. After George III was prayed for in the Catholic church at Hexam as late as 1780, Jacobite-minded spinsters would leave their seats and walk out at the mention of his name. There is a story, probably legendary, that at the coronation of the third Hanoverian monarch Prince Charles was actually present. It is likely that the tale has its origin in another report. When the herald read out the customary challenge, inviting anyone who contested the crowning to come forward, a white glove was thrown down by some Jacobite sympathiser. One wonders whether he or she had received private instructions from Prince Charles to do this.

'What can a bird do that has not found a right nest? He must flit from bough to bough.' The wandering Prince scribbled these melancholy words on a scrap of paper. For him there was no right nest, no coming back, but in Scottish hearts his reign is never-ending and secure.

It is now publickly said that the young P—r himself came from Flanders to see the Coronation, that he was in Westminster Abbey during the Coronation, and in town two or three days before, and after it, under the name of Mr Brown, and being asked by a gentleman who knew him abroad, how he durst venture hither, his answer was, that he was very safe.

 From a letter in *The Gazetteer* quoted in an article in *The Edinburgh Advertiser* of January 6th, 1764

Charles made an excursion to London in September 1750 for five days, during which time he drank tea with Dr King, a staunch Jacobite, at his house in Red Lion Square, and visited Lady Primrose, a powerful ally, who had offered a warm reception to Flora Macdonald after her liberation from prison. He also occupied himself with paving the way for a future rising, and, in order to keep his memory before the public, he distributed cheap trinkets among those jewellers who lived in hidden corners of the town, and were in greater contact with the colony of Jacobites.

These tawdry trifles consisted principally of seals, rings and watch-cases, on some of which were engraved a small likeness of the Prince; but as there were no initials or inscriptions, the engravers were able to assert that they were fancy heads. On some of the seals there was a motto, 'Look, love, and follow', and these words could equally be declared void of double meaning save for those who were initiated in the intrigues which were still rife.

From *A Court in Exile*
by Marchese Vitelleschi

I never used the word Pretender, which is a most unseemly word, in my life, unless (God help me) I was obliged to take the oaths of Abjuration and Supremacy at elections and so forth, and even then I always did it with a qualm of conscience. Seriously I am very glad I did not live in 1745, for though as a lawyer I could not have pleaded Charles's right, and as a clergyman I could not have prayed for him, yet as a soldier I would I am sure, against the convictions of my better reason, have fought for him to the bottom of the gallows.

Sir Walter Scott in a letter to a friend

The Prince kept himself privet for some days in Paris, until he got cloaths made, for he arrived in the same equipage yt he was in the Highlands, wch cou'd not be worse, he had not a second shirt nor a stoken to his foot but what those gents yt were aboard gave him, & to those yt were with him. He was in a frightfull condition as those gents says when he arrived aboard the ships, not only his feet all cut & stript, but his legs and thyes in ulsers, even worse than he was when Sullivan quitted him. When the Prince was cload, his Rags were looked upon as so many reliques, there were a great many disputes & quarrells about them, not only among the Kings subjects, but the Frinch, especially the Ladys. Every one thought to have as much right as another, to his depouil, one wou'd have one thing, another anoth thing, in short they were divided as well as it cou'd be; one had his bonnet, one his Coat, another the old Shoose & Stokens another his pipe &ca but there were some still dissatisfied, there was nothing left but the wig, wch was a most abominable one, but a Lady discover'd it was not given away, but thrown aside, & she wou'd have it. She was told it wou'd infect her, yt it was full of vermine, as really it was, & never such a one was set to frighten Crows away, but she got it, & set it up pretiously, as the rest was by those yt had them.

 Taken from the Stuart Papers at Windsor by Royal permission: *The Narrative of John William O'Sullivan, one of the Seven Men of Moidart*

Prince Charles Edward Stuart, from the portrait at Townley
Hall, reproduced by courtesy of *Country Life*

Return to the Borderland . . . nourished on ballad lore, the spirit
of the Borderer can always travel its green byways in memory

RETURN TO THE BORDERLAND

by Jane Oliver

CUSTOM frets the finest fabric threadbare. But the sharp knife of crisis can slit up the seams and reveal it, for an inch or an instant, in its first splendour. Crisis is timeless. A lifetime can lie, it seems, between two strokes of the clock, and perception, heightened sufficiently by danger, joy or grief, break through the time barrier as aircraft now break through the lesser barrier of sound, entering a new order of reality.

It is fifteen years ago now since I made that discovery in an ambulance station in Central London during the blitz. We used to sit there with the lights flickering and the building shaking round us like a dog coming out of the water. Tension mounted as the telephone bell rang again and again, and one ambulance after another roared off into the pandemonium outside. At the next telephone call I must slam my feet into gum-boots, clap a tin hat on my head and hurry to the control room for particulars of the incident at which I was required.

Moonlight nights, they were, with the barrage balloons poised overhead like a shoal of immense pewter money-box pigs for giants' children, the sky opening and shutting in a wildfire blaze of ack-ack, flares like candelabra swinging from the roof of hell, and over all the unforgettable double drone of the enemy bombers that occasionally flickered like shining minnows between the searchlights' long, groping fingers.

The same moon, I used to think, will be shining over the hills of the Borderland. It used to be the moonless nights that meant trouble there. Men mustered round the gaunt peels, in leather jacks or blackened mail, with steel caps dulled for fear a gleam should betray their wearers. Bridles chimed, and the waters of the fords churned white under their horses' hooves as the contingent crossed the Border. Then came the yells of combat, the clash of swords, the roaring blaze of fired ricks, the frightened complaint of sheep and cattle driven along unfamiliar ways.

But it will be quiet there now. So quiet. A sheep will bleat, perhaps, or an owl call, the small sounds loud in that blessed peace. The burns will mutter to themselves like old men talking in their sleep. As the ambulance station shuddered or a near miss came screaming down I deliberately steadied myself for an effort of will too definite to be considered mere daydream or reverie. In all but the material sense, I returned to the Border-land.

My body remained, indeed, in the bare, brilliant room with its racks of gas-proof clothing, its pegs for tin hats and first-aid satchels, a row of gum-boots backed against the wall below. But I, I myself, as nearly free from time, perhaps, as I shall ever be until the hour of my death, walked once again up the hill road that wound past the patchwork of little fields in Liddesdale to the fell and the moor beyond. Below me, innocent in the moon-light, lay the sleeping valley in which I had been born, the smoke from a few late fires scribbled against the dark bulk of the woods on the far side of the river.

The river itself was as I remembered it, spreading here and there into a silver shield, splintering elsewhere into bright shards among the shallows. I had waded up it so often as a child that I knew every useful, overhanging alder by which I could haul myself over each treacherously sleek stone.

They were all there still, no longer wan under the moon as time relaxed its grip, but brilliant in the sunshine of all my remembered summers. Once more I waded thigh-deep beside the overhanging banks, clotted with meadowsweet and astir with butterflies, once more the gnats moved in a droning cloud about me and the dippers curtseyed on their stones. Because the river-bed was sharply stony we wore sandshoes as we worked our way up it, our smocks tucked out of the way inside the elastic of our drawers.

There they were, shallows and pool, wood and river, miraculously inviolate in a world so savaged by noise that it was difficult to believe in quietness any more. Standing, by a supreme effort of will, beside the river, or at the end of the hill road on the moor, the flaring malice of fires that striped the London streets wasp-like between darkness and glare seemed remote. But sometimes it was harder to escape. Then I murmured the names of the hills that stood round Liddesdale like an incantation till they slowly rose about me, under the same moon.

'Roan Fell, Hartsgarth, Din Fell, Arnton, Larriston, Blinkbonny Height, Tinnis Hill. . . . ' So men, long ago, chalked circles on the ground, inscribed them with mighty angelic names and withdrew within them against the attacks of the creatures of the Pit. So, standing in thought within the circle of the Border hills the spirit was so safe that the fate of the body scarcely mattered.

'I will lift up mine eyes unto the hills. . . . ' How many generations of our forefathers, living, fighting or hiding in the Borderland, have evoked the protection of these round-shouldered, tawny heights? And how few of them, in their wildest dreams, could ever have imagined a crisis as strange as that in which their descendant evoked their protection once more. The need for protection, however, would scarcely have surprised them. Fugitives from invading armies, broken men who had deserted from our own, freedom-loving men of the Covenant, all knew these hills.

For the Borderland lay in the path of every English army which, since the Romans built their great wall from sea to sea and gave up the subjection of those to the north of it as a bad job, ever tried to get the better of its Scottish neighbours. From the Borders men joined the armies of the great liberator, Robert the Bruce, as he drove southwards to complete the work so astonishingly done at Bannockburn. Some of the fairest flowers of the Border were among those 'wede awa' at Flodden, and Prince Charles Edward passed through Liddesdale to the disastrous ebb-tide of his affairs at Derby. There is a legend that he slept at Larriston, and a mound is still pointed out as the resting-place of one of his followers who died by the wayside and was laid in 'the Hielandman's Grave'.

And yet, there is more to the Border folk than stubborn strength and obstinate lawlessness. Their imagination has a lyric quality as sharply sweet as the cloud-berries which grow on the summits of their hills. It is scarcely surprising that their contribution to literature should be considerable. From the

Borderland come the songs of Robert Burns, the monumental epics of Sir Walter Scott, some of the metrical psalms and paraphrases which recall a time when the traditions of the Scottish Kirk were maintained at the risk of their lives by men and women who could not read and learned all they sang by heart. And, above all, there are the Ballads.

The Ballads express the singing soul of the Borderland. Composed for the most part by unknown men and women centuries ago, they have been handed down by word of mouth from generation to generation, gaining here a little and there a little, the memorial of a people who lived, as it were, on the edge of the unseen. Many things which we in our modern scientific complacency might consider incredible would not surprise them in the least. Those who sang:

> Kilmeny has been she cannot tell where,
> Kilmeny has seen what she cannot declare,

might hardly raise an eyebrow at the sight of one of their descendants in tin hat and gum boots fording the Kershope beside them one moonlight night. The Ballads are full of the stories of those who came and went between worlds.

> It fell about the Martinmas,
>   When nights are lang and mirk,
> The carline wife's three sons came hame,
>   And their hats were o the birk.
> It neither grew in syke nor ditch,
>   Nor yet in ony sheugh;
> But at the gates o Paradise
>   That birk grew fair eneugh. . . .

And Thomas the Rhymer, bewitched by its Queen, visited Elfland, that twilight realm between earth and hell, which paid tribute of a fair young man or maiden to hell every seven years and was more dreadfully associated with our own world.

> O they rade on and farther on,
>   And they waded through red blude to the knee,
> For a' the blude that's shed on earth
>   Rins through the springs o that countrie.

Surely the rivers of Elfland must have run in spate in our time. And yet, terrible as our wars have been, the Borderland has long since endured, again and again, the utmost destruction the weapons available to her enemies permitted. Such leaders as Surrey, Hertford and Dacre unhesitatingly gutted her glorious Abbeys and burned her towns. Had modern facilities been at their disposal no doubt they would not have left one stone upon another. What they left undone, the Reformers, at the full-swing of reaction from Romish superstition, considered it their incredible duty to do. And yet, in spite of them all, we can still find peace beside the gentle grey ghost of Dryburgh, see Melrose glow like a rose in stone, walk between the fire-scarred walls of heroic Kelso and Jedburgh.

We must admit that in our own time the Borderland has also suffered, though more subtly, from her friends. We have permitted the pollution of her rivers by the waste from our mills, gouged tunnels and cut railways out of her hillsides, watched the towns drain the life of the countryside from her quiet valleys. The humbler ruins of the shepherd's but and ben, the once-musical smithy, now take their place in attendance on the nobler ghosts of the Border Abbeys and once impregnable strongholds of Roxburgh, Hermitage, Newark, Neidpath, who precede them into the shades.

And yet there are signs that the swallowing up of our people by the cities may not be irrevocable. Far-sighted mill owners are establishing subsidiary workrooms which offer girls employment in their own villages, so that the need to earn a livelihood shall not compel them to leave home. Let the denuded countryside endure her winter with patience. It may well be that in the fullness of time her exiles will return, having known the cities of the world and the clamour thereof, emerging from the hubbub with a new capacity for appreciating her silence, just broken by the blessed country sounds.

There are many ways of returning to the Borderland besides the one I first chose fifteen years ago. Perhaps the best method of travelling is still the old pilgrim's way, rucksack on back and staff in hand. There is much to be said, too, for making the journey on horseback. Queen Mary spurred from Jedburgh to Hermitage and back nearly four hundred years ago, and Sir Walter Scott jogged into Liddesdale before there was a road for his carriage. There is also something to be said, unexpectedly, for piloting a light aircraft over it, as I did before the war.

Not for anything would I have missed seeing at a glance the whole countryside into which the Solway thrusts like a sword, the hills folding about the lovely valleys, each different and yet part of one whole: Ettrick and Yarrow, Eskdale, Teviot, and Liddesdale.

One realizes then that though so much changes, more remains unchanged. Seen from above, the alien elements recede. It may be that distance and time can mellow even Blake's 'dark, Satanic mills'. There was a time when no man crossed the Border without weapons by his side, unless, like such immortals as Sir William Wallace, they crossed it in chains. That is something, maybe, to set against our losses. It seemed a great deal, those moonlight nights when I took refuge from hell let loose by returning to the Borderland.

Moonlight is kind as a lover to that countryside. It hides the unlovely pylons and telegraph poles that march across the hills, bearing the twentieth century's amenities to mill and manse, cottage and village hall. In its light the great swathes of conifers with which the Forestry Commission has eclipsed so many of John Buchan's 'lion-coloured hills' lose their militaristic precision and wrap themselves like a douce dark shawl round the shoulders of the old land.

Across the valley, or is it across the years, sounds the heavenly trumpet of the All Clear. From the summit of Roan Fell the curlew's spring call tumbles in a cascade of sheer joy.

Time is . . . time was . . . There is no time . .

Let anyone walk across a Border moorland on one of those days not uncommon in the district, when, overhead and all around, the sky is shrouded by grey clouds, peaceable and motionless, piled in masses high and imposing. As this is generally in late autumn, let him notice also that the bent is brown, and the heather-bloom beginning to fade, and that the grey tint on the sky is helped by the same colour on rock and stone, and then let him watch the effect of this on pool and stream, and he will feel and understand the force, truthfulness, and beauty of the expression—*the wan water*. The stream which was formerly bright and sparkling, has taken on the tint of the landscape around it, and we feel that it now touches the eye and heart with its wan look. The older minstrels noted aspects of the scenery of this description; and they did more, they instinctively fused these with the story in hand, or with some turn in it. The particular look, for example, of the stream is introduced with wonderful effect into several of the historical ballads. It occurs in *The Douglas Tragedy* already quoted. And mark its peculiar appropriateness. The hero of the ballad has carried off his love after a deadly conflict, in which the father and brothers of the maiden fell. The hero and his love ride slowly across the hills between the Yarrow and the Tweed, amid a quiet sheen of moonlight all over the vague weird-like moorland; the father and brothers are lying dead in the deep glen of the mountain burn which the lovers have left behind them. The companion of the maiden begins to feel that he too has carried with him a wound—in fact his death-wound—from the conflict. The dying man finds it necessary to rest, and the minstrel with a wonderful touch tells us:

> O they rade on, and on they rade,
> And a' by the licht of the moon,
> Until they cam to yon wan water,
> And there they lichted doun.

Where more appropriately could a dying man, with fading hope and sense, have rested than by the 'wan water'?

John Veitch: *The History and Poetry of the Scottish Border*

47

As some atonement for their laxity of morals on most occasions, the Borderers were severe observers of the faith which they had pledged, even to an enemy. If any person broke his word so plighted, the individual to whom faith had not been observed used to bring to the next Border meeting a glove hung on the point of a spear, and proclaim to Scots and English the name of the defaulter. This was accounted so great a disgrace to all connected with him, that his own clansmen sometimes destroyed him to escape the infamy he had brought on them.

Constable, a spy engaged by Sir Ralph Sadler, talks of two Border thieves whom he used as his guides: 'That they would not care to steal, and yet that they would not betray any man that trusts in them, for all the gold in Scotland or in France. They are my guides and outlaws. If they would betray me they might get their pardons, and cause me to be hanged; but I have tried them ere this.'

Sir Walter Scott, in a note to The Monastery

SCOTTISH HILLS:
AN EXPLORER'S APPRECIATION

by Tom Weir

' . . . A TRUE mountain country, aloof from lowlands, but within
sight and sound of the sea. There is spaciousness here. Light
and colour are always changing on hill and water. One is conscious of the continual movement of nature, in the sea, in running
water and in the wind that drives the clouds before it in procession across the sky. In winter Atlantic gales and furious
volleys of rain or sudden splintering hail keep the air alive and
exciting. . . .

'Here our mountains are small, but they are steep-sided, individual in colour, form and texture. They stand proudly in their
own right. Clouds sweep over them. Snow turns them white.
In fact as I see it they are true mountains. Half an hour's walk
up the hill-side and we change the world about us in all its
perspective. Seaward the Summer Isles are spread like a chart
below. Away to the west across the Minch lies the long horizon
of the Hebrides. On a clear day the peaks of the Cuillin can be
picked out seventy miles to the south-west. The whole eastern
sky-line is of mainland mountains. They start with the rugged
sandstone bosses of Torridon; then Slioch, over against Loch
Maree; and above Gruinard Bay rise the spikes of An Teallach.
The five tops of Coigach build a massy block in the south-east.
Then comes Stack Polly with its cockscomb crest and strange
lobster claws of rock; the crown of Cul Mor and the massive
Atlantic watch-tower of Suilven. These peaks guard a wide
sanctuary of moor and loch of which over 100 square miles is
uninhabited. No man sleeps there. Beyond Edrachillis Bay rise
the hills behind Scourie; and beyond those we can see nearly to

49

Cape Wrath. And then behold the sky, an hundred miles of it. So many things going on at once; clouds of every pattern with play of colour on sea and land; here bright sunlight, there a black storm. An enchanted land.

'So I have come back there to live.'

Thus does Dr Tom Longstaff write of Coigach in Wester Ross after thirteen adventurous chapters packed with exciting description which he calls *This My Voyage*, his voyage having taken him to the Alps some twenty times, then to the Caucasus, east to the Garhwal Himalaya, north to Tibet, south to Nepal and Everest, west to the Karakorum and Hindu Kush, then over to the New World to the Rockies, and up to the Arctic regions of Spitzbergen and Greenland. It is a breathless book, spun with glittering threads from the gold of fifty volumes of diaries dealing with a life lived at the full; the book of a man who has taught himself to see, and who has chosen to live the remainder of his life in the Highlands of Scotland.

I cannot begin to class myself with Tom Longstaff, but my excuse for writing this is that I too have had the good fortune to travel around a bit, in some cases to the same ranges of the Himalaya, to Yugoslavia and the Central Alps, to Arctic Norway, Nepal; and it is from the point of view of my own voyage that I am going to try to tell you how I feel about Scottish hills after twenty-five years of varied mountaineering at home and abroad. And to do this properly I have to take you back with me quite a distance, otherwise you will not be able to distinguish truth from sentiment.

You have to look at me as a tenement-dweller in Glasgow, a fifteen-year-old apprentice athirst for adventure like every other boy, but with only one Sunday of each week and a fortnight each year to satisfy what was regarded as a strange craving for the wilds. To be condemned to live in Glasgow and never see the wide world was a sentence too terrible to contemplate. So my escape was books, the Himalaya, the Arctic, the Antarctic, the Andes, the Alps. But I can date when life really began for me by the purchase of a bicycle, when I discovered the Campsie Fells which range ten miles to the north of the town.

It was spring, I remember, when I climbed them, and saw to my amazement range upon range of snow peaks filling the northern horizon. I had been to the Highlands once, but no one had told me of the proximity of these peaks to my very doorstep, or so it seemed to me with a bicycle; and thereupon I resolved that I would climb every top, find out the best ways of getting to them; buy a tent and a stove, and discover what lay beyond.

And that was exactly what I did. I knew no one who shared my interests. In fact I did not feel the need of a companion. Nothing could hold me indoors. Summer nights I would be on the Campsies, thinking nothing of the twenty miles' cycle run or the uphill dash, so long as I got on to the rocks and explored new ways up the face, or sat on the top at sunset to look on the promised land of mountains stretching to the north.

I tell you this because, although I did not appreciate it then, the mountains of Scotland were my Himalaya, and nothing that has come to me anywhere abroad can equal the days of discovery on our own homeland hills, which is why Scotland will always be first in my affection.

How tremendously these years of discovery yielded up! I had climbed Buachaille Etive Mor in rain and mist by a rock face that struck terror into my heart; had camped in the heart of the Black Mount; had spent a week in Torridon with a new-found companion of vast experience who at twenty-six years of age seemed a veritable grey-beard, and such was the impression of that holiday that to this day the colour and form of these magnificent mountains as they were then remains brighter than the memory left over from last year.

But I still preferred spending my holidays alone, rather than with companions, partly because I wanted the feeling of isolation, which to me with my wee tent was so important, and partly because I felt all my impressions sharpened by being alone, particularly up in the mist traversing a ridge, compass in hand, when there might be a sudden revelation of silvery lochs, or ranges of sunlit mountains, and what had seemed a grim battle was transformed, the mist dispersing as so many cloud fleeces or playing hide-and-seek with the ridge in the most delightful way.

Then there were the friendships I struck up with families isolated in lonely glens—people with whom I still keep in touch, and whose houses are second home to me. Where else on earth could one get such a welcome and such warm hospitality as with these people? Unfortunately, though, all too many of the old people I knew have died, and the boys and girls have left the old home to work in Glasgow or London.

What I do find about Scotland now is that mountaineering for its own sake does not seem to matter so much. Once upon a time it was the tops and the climb that mattered, almost to the exclusion of all else. Nowadays it is the uniqueness of Scotland I appreciate—the subtlety of its colours, the character of its glens, the individuality of its sea lochs, the wealth of its bird life, the fun to be had on its islands—even an island like Eigg which has only one little mountain, but so much else.

And yet, perhaps because I have more time, or have a better knowledge of where to look, I seem to find more and more rock faces to explore. For example last year I had a fortnight in Ross and Sutherland. We went to Torridon first, to stay in a little cottage at the foot of Liathach, now leased to the Scottish Mountaineering Club, and wonderfully situated for exploring Choire Mhic Fhearchair, a wild recess in the north side of Beinn Eighe where three slender pillars of pale quartz stand on a pedestal of red Torridonian sandstone in a total cliff of 1,000 feet. Mountaineers have made difficult routes on these pillars, but no one had yet climbed the connecting walls between them, and our ambition was to be the first to do so. We achieved it too, by getting three splendid routes in three days, each taking us into a fantastic realm of rock scenery.

The climbs were good, but perhaps even better than the climbing to me was the feeling of being back home, to a terrain which is almost in my bones—a wild country, as wild as any in Scotland, but for me who know every inch of it, a friendly country dotted with lochans, each of which is a winking friendly eye, and where I know I can find bobbing sandpipers, or a pair of greenshank, or the nesting island of a black throated diver, or look into a corrie where I know the rare dwarf cornel grows.

Then, by way of contrast, we exchanged in a day the striking mountain forms of Torridon for the peaks of the Reay, the bleakest and loneliest hills in Scotland, that lie above Cape Wrath and plunge to the sea in the greatest cliff on the mainland of Scotland called Clo Mor. We camped on the daisy-studded machair of Durness and drove each day ten miles to our peaks in preference to camping in the grim heart of Reay.

A climber surveys his lonely dominion, high on the central ridge
of Aonach Dubh

Winter on the high tops: in the upper picture the climbers have reached the summit of Ben Lui. Below are Inverness-shire peaks from Creag Petridh, above Loch Laggan

My interest here was in the great cliff called Creag Dionard which sits above a black and lonely loch two hours walk from the public road, a face 1,000 feet high yet possessing to that date no route up its steepest parts. Here the rock is quartz, hard and flinty-white, sound to climb on, and the two routes we made were pure delight, likewise two others we made on a slender 600 foot rock pyramid called A' Gheir Gorm, a miniature Buachaille Etive Mor.

Our days were not solely devoted to climbing. By the sea we looked at birds and found nests; and on Clo Mor we looked down 900 feet of space to the boiling sea, where millions of sea birds buzzed hither and thither like so many bees, straight-winged fulmars, scurrying puffins, while every ledge of that dizzy cliff seemed to be packed with courting guillemots or razorbills, or kittiwakes, or shags.

Scotland strikes me now as being a place with so much to see that I am extremely reluctant to leave it. Where, for example, can skiing and an interest in natural history be so perfectly balanced as in the Cairngorms in springtime, when in April and May the great snowfields of spring snow are wonderful for fast running, and snow buntings and ptarmigan are busy with their courtship. The dotterel have arrived, the golden plover sounds once again on the tops, and if you know where to look, the golden eagle is with young. Then in June there are the little arctic flowers, blooming wherever the terrain is favourable: clumps of cushion pink; or purple, gold, or starry saxifrages; alpine lady's mantle; or sprays of roseroot—each a joy to the eye on these bare tops.

I have skied for a few years now, in Norway, in Austria, and in the high Alps, but the most memorable days of my life have been in Scotland, particularly after storm, when the fury of blizzards in which no man could live had been succeeded by windless calm, when every tree was encased in feathers and the low January sun shone with blue light.

Then Scotland was transformed. Truly an Arctic land, where only the lochs gleamed to break an expanse vast as Tibet and even more sparsely populated, where the only means of locomotion was on skis, and those so equipped wore a pair of magic slippers that swished so lightly through the silky powder that it was like moving in space.

53

Nor is this such an isolated happening. Two days before writing this I was on Green Lowther near Leadhills, which vies with Tomintoul for the honour of being the highest village in Scotland. The world was of calm Arctic beauty, no wind, warm sun, with the domes of the hills shining silvery against a sky of brittle blue.

Out of sight of the village we were in another world, of untracked snow and softly moulded hills where little knots of hungry sheep pawed at the drifts to find only frozen ground underneath. We climbed to the tops to look over the swelling hills of Galloway, a range like the Cairngorms, dimpled with corries, mile upon mile of them, and I realised with a shock that I had only climbed one of them. So much to do, so much to see in Scotland, and so little time to see it. And that brings me to a point that makes me think. What is the best way of spending my remaining time on earth, now that I am forty-one years of age? Is it to keep climbing while I am young enough to do the hard routes, or should I obey an inclination I have to learn more about nature by studying it in all its aspects, birds, plants, animals, people, things? Scotland as a country is surely as worthy of study as Scotland merely as a place in which to climb.

I might decide, but fate I fear would take the decision out of my hands, because along would come a spring day, ideal for watching the arrival of bird migrants, or studying something of social import, but ideal also for forcing a way up the northeast face of Ben Nevis whose ridges because of their length and accumulation of winter snow give the most alpine climbing in Scotland.

Last year I went to Nevis on such a day, a morning of keen frost, snow cornices glistening against the hard blue of the sky, the sheen of ice shadowy in the gullies, and invitation to climb shouting from the three greatest ridges in Britain, each offering a challenge of wine-red rocks plastered high up with snow and ice.

Could any one of them be climbed in its present condition? Not until you have had a try do you pronounce judgment, but we felt they could, so we chose the hardest, the Observatory Ridge, the narrowest and steepest of the Nevis ridges, and such was the day and such our luck when we found most of the steps already cut for us by a previous party, that we climbed it in two hours. So we descended the second of the great ridges, called Tower Ridge. Two climbs in one day, very nice, but we still felt cheated of a really hard climb, so when we noticed that Slingsby's Chimney was snow-filled and contained at least one ice pitch we crossed over to it and climbed it, finishing up the North-east Buttress, to arrive on the summit feeling we had done more than an Alpine day, and so we had with more than 6,000 feet of icy rock climbing.

Weariness was cast aside when we sat down by the indicator and let our eyes roam over the mighty panorama of snow-flecked hills beneath our gaze. No need to pin-point them one by one. The old friends stood out and reached out their hands to us from Ross, Sutherland, Perth, Argyll, Inverness, Stirling; not mere individuals but ranges like the Cuillin, crowding round and for-ever entangled in our hearts, calling to us that we were home—and surely we knew there was no place like it.

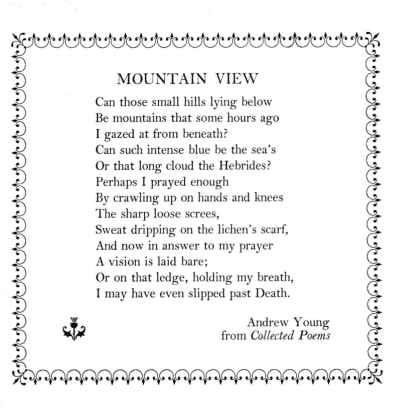

MOUNTAIN VIEW

Can those small hills lying below
Be mountains that some hours ago
I gazed at from beneath?
Can such intense blue be the sea's
Or that long cloud the Hebrides?
Perhaps I prayed enough
By crawling up on hands and knees
The sharp loose screes,
Sweat dripping on the lichen's scarf,
And now in answer to my prayer
A vision is laid bare;
Or on that ledge, holding my breath,
I may have even slipped past Death.

Andrew Young
from *Collected Poems*

At five o'clock we stepped on to the summit and passed, as it were, into another realm. Far beneath our feet a mighty expanse of tawny hills and plains stretched to the utmost fringes of the earth, and faded there in unfathomable blue. Over all hung the breathless hush of evening. One heard it circle the world like a lapping tide, the wave-beat of the sea of beauty; and as we listened from our watch-tower and looked out across the broad earth, our own little lives and our flush of triumph in climbing a new route became very trivial things. They were suddenly measured for us against eternity and the real, and in such perspective vanished away, of no moment. Yet in that same instant our climb to the granite crags, the bare summit and the lands below, were with ourselves idealized as though in a point out of time and exalted in oneness. We began to understand a little less darkly, what it may mean to inherit the earth.

On the summit of Lochnagar
from *Mountaineering in Scotland* by W. H. Murray

Up and up we went, digging, hitting, carving, moving steadily and without interruption for an hour. Quite suddenly, the snow became firm and reliable. On our left hand, stark square-cut towers were silhouetted against the starry sky, and round them could be heard a mighty rushing of winds, the voice of the high and lonely places of the earth. Then Zero Gully broadened out and debouched without cornice on the summit plateau. We went over the top one by one, our hearts filled with relief. The time was eleven-thirty p.m.

'Well,' said Mackenzie, 'we're up.'

I answered 'Thank God!' And for once I meant it. Nothing more was said, then or later. But I had no doubt then, and have none now, that this was the longest and hardest climb in relation to sheer strain that we should ever do. We had learnt that when one stands on the summit after such a climb it is not the mountain that is conquered—we have conquered self and the mountain has helped us.

Ben Nevis: Observatory Ridge in Winter
Ib d.

Even in Edinburgh, the same spirit (of hospitality) runs through the common people; who are infinitely more civil, humanized, and hospitable, than any I ever met with. Every one is ready to serve and assist a stranger; they shew the greatest respect to a person superior to them; and you never receive an impertinent answer. . . .

I have continued in this City ever since you last heard from me, and find it so agreeable that I foresee it will be with difficulty I shall prevail upon myself to leave it. The inhabitants have so much civility and hospitality, and the favours I receive are so many, that it would argue a want of acknowledgment, and that I am unworthy of the good opinion they are so kind to entertain, did I wish to hasten my departure. . . . I find here everything I can wish; and must own, I never spent my time more to my satisfaction. The gentlemen of this nation (pardon my impartiality) are infinitely better calculated for an agreeable society than Englishmen; as they have the spirit of the French without their grimace, with much more learning, and more modest, mixed with philosophic reserve. They are extremely fond of jovial company; and if they did not too often sacrifice to Bacchus the joys of a vacant hour, they would be the most entertaining people in Europe: but the goodness of their wine, and the severity of their climate, are indeed some excuse for them.

Captain Topham: *Letters from Edinburgh,* 1774

58

SCOTTISH HOSPITALITY

by Moray McLaren

ALL the world knows that the Scots are mean; and all the world
also knows that they are amongst the most hospitable people in
Europe. There is no point in trying to resolve the contradiction
of these two reputations. The one is based upon an undoubted
habit of mind or of manner amongst certain Scots; the other
rests upon an undoubted, well-established and internationally
recognized fact.

Our history has been that of a poor country. This has tended
to make us penny-wise, an understandable failing compensated
for by romantic outbursts of pound-folly. The world which is
inclined to remember a man's weaknesses rather than his good
qualities has noted only our penny-wisdom and called it mean-
ness. It has been compelled, though not always with pleasure,
to recognize our unreserved hospitality.

I say 'not always with pleasure' because it must be admitted
that sometimes, but only sometimes, we tend to overdo this
pleasure of ours, for pleasure it undoubtedly is. More often
(and it is agreeable to notice this in past accounts) we succeed
in giving pleasure while taking it.

A poor but proud and essentially warm-hearted people living
upon the fringe of Europe takes naturally to the pleasure of
giving hospitality as soon as it can. It satisfies pride, exercises
the warm heart and is not too deeply damaging to the resources.
The eighteenth century, when at last the poor but proud and
warm-hearted Scots found themselves at internal peace, with
some external relations and a reasonable hope of prosperity,
was the first time when they could really gain an international
reputation for hospitality: and they certainly gained it.

This was the century when the learned men of Europe regarded Edinburgh as the most important city in Britain and as the one most worthy of a pilgrimage. It was also the century of the heaviest eating and deepest drinking, amongst any classes above the mildly well-to-do level, that our country has ever known. It may well be imagined then that the flood-gates of Scottish hospitality were opened in the eighteenth century in a way which made a deep and lasting impression.

Some travellers found the experience of Edinburgh and Scottish hospitality overpowering. Not all the dishes, such as rizzard haddies, haggis and sheep's head were to southern tastes. The wine, however, in particular the claret, found general favour. Though here again the habit of sitting long over the glasses after the ladies had left the dining-room was pushed to an extent unknown even in England where drinking was deeper and more concentrated than on the Continent.

This was the century in which Boswell and four companions could get through thirty modern pints of claret and hock and nearly half a dozen bottles of spirits in one evening. It was also a period when for the first time travellers were regularly visiting the south of Scotland and Edinburgh in particular. There is ample evidence that, as with the visitors in *Humphry Clinker*, some were amused, delighted by the evident desire of the Scots that all who came to them should share to the full in the gargantuan feasts, some also fell by the wayside, or more accurately, beneath the board.

Country hospitality in the Lowlands, though less frequently displayed, simply because of lack of opportunity, was no less open-hearted and overwhelming. The occasions of it, too, lasted longer than in the towns. When lairds or farmers entertained their neighbours, their guests often had to come from the surrounding countryside over land that in the south would have been thought near impassable by daylight, and which even here was more than could conveniently be managed by returning revellers after dark. It was the custom then when one asked a guest to dinner to ask him for the night. Sometimes there were scarcely enough bedrooms to accommodate all the guests; but this did not matter. The dinner party would continue all night. There are stories of entertainments of this kind that lasted two or even three days with the guests doing no more than leaving and returning to the board in relays. It would be an impertinence to attempt to re-tell here some of the admirable stories which Dean Ramsay tells of this kind of hospitality at this period. The reader is, however, referred to his classic book, *Reminiscences of Scottish Life and Character*.

I cannot resist, however, the pleasure of setting down once again an extract from the anecdotes of, of all people, that sentimental eighteenth century Scottish writer Henry Mackenzie, author of *The Man of Feeling*. It shows what was regarded as ordinary drinking in the capital of Scotland at the time. And, by inference, it gives us an idea of what some of Scotland's guests may then have been expected to support in the way of hospitality: some of them may even have enjoyed it:

'It is dangerous to the health of an old man accustomed to drink hard to give up drinking suddenly. An old friend of mine shewed good sense in this. He was one of the hardest drinkers in Scotland in his middle-age, having prepared himself, however, by having tasted no strong liquor till past twenty. From that till sixty he drank more than any man in Scotland. I once saw him after he had drunk fourteen bottles of punch when he came to my father's to supper, and, feeling his situation, begged to lie down for half-an-hour while the company was playing cards. He was called when supper was served and behaved with perfect propriety like a gentleman. After sixty he reduced pint by pint until he had only a few glasses poured out by his wife. He lived to over four score.'

What echoes of this heroic past still linger in our hospitality today? Well, I think there can be no doubt that we still exert ourselves more than does any other part of Britain (and even of Ireland) in our attempts to entertain our visitors. We do not have the vast appetites or the enormous thirsts that our forefathers possessed—nor the means to satisfy them, but it would be safe to say that there can be few countries in Europe in which it would be more difficult for a stranger to go hungry and thirsty.

Despite our capricious climate, despite our foolish and restrictive licensing laws, particularly on Sunday, despite the catering wages regulations imposed upon us by those at Westminster who are accustomed to London conditions and are ignorant of Scottish ones, despite these and other drawbacks, it is Scottish hospitality which is most frequently praised by our post-war visitors. I am not sure that some of the most abiding memories that those who come to the Festival take away with them are not of the artistic feasts that they have enjoyed but the purely private and personal ones that they have partaken of in people's houses.

We are still, even in these days of air travel, comparatively remote. We still lie upon the fringe of Europe on the road to more or less nowhere. We are still, by the counting of heads, far from being a rich country. And, above all, we still like to be visited and like to be liked. So we remain as we were (though on a less heroic scale) amongst the most hospitable people in Europe.

Lest this should seem too boastful a way of ending this article, let me remind any reader who has gone this far with me that I have pointed out the drawbacks and discomforts of being entertained by the Scots as well as the delights.

Among the ancient Scots it was deemed infamous in a man to have the door of his house shut, lest, as the bards express it, 'the stranger should come and behold his contracted soul'. The free and open hospitality which characterizes a primitive condition of society survived much later in Scotland, and particularly in the Highlands, than in the more highly civilized countries of Europe. Fynes Morison, a graduate of Cambridge, who visited Scotland in 1598, tells us that he noticed no regular inns with signs hanging out, but that private householders would entertain passengers on entreaty or where acquaintance was claimed. The last statement is interestingly corroborated in the account of his journey to Scotland which that eccentric genius, John Taylor, the Thames waterman (commonly known as the Water-poet) printed in 1618. In the course of what he terms his 'Pennyless Pilgrimage, or Moneyless Perambulation', he claims to have depended entirely on private hospitality. Everywhere, indeed, in his progress through Scotland, he appears to have been feasted sumptuously, and liberally supplied with money by hospitable gentlemen who probably found his witty conversation ample recompense.

F. Marian McNeill: *The Scots Kitchen*

ROYAL PEARLS

by Marie W. Stuart

LIKE the Princess of Serendip who was so lucky in what she found while looking for something else, I was always on a different quest when stray scraps of this story would catch my eye; so pocketing them thriftily, now here, now there, I gathered a fankle of threads that wove in and out of four centuries. Now I can sort them out and knot them together, winding all up to run after this fashion: ~

We do not know what cunning traders slowly collected and matched the pearls which were to form so memorable a necklace nor what skilled craftsmen first strung them into ropes of beauty, but their verifiable story begins in 1533 when a marriage was arranged between François I's son, the Duke of Orleans, and the fourteen-year-old Catherine de Medici. Since the French viewed this as a *mésalliance* with a *parvenue* it was necessary for her family to send the bride to her new country with as sumptuous a dowry and trousseau as possible. Catherine's half-brother, Alessandro de Medici, on learning that she was in that unhappiest feminine predicament of having nothing fit to wear, determined to do his best on her behalf. With princely guile he announced that he was planning to improve the defences of Florence and for that purpose he levied a tax of 5,000 crowns on the citizens, a sum which he calmly diverted to buy the jewels and rich silks and velvets with which his sister might impress the French court. Among these treasures were the pearls that she took to France and wore as a merry if not beautiful *dauphine* and later as Queen when her motto, 'I bring light and serenity' was proving to be a mockery as her sinister character developed only too rapidly.

The years passed and on the marriage of her son François

in 1559 Catherine presented the ropes of pearls to another foreign bride, the youthful Mary, Queen of Scots, for whose father she herself had once been suggested as a wife. It must have been a grudging gift for they say that Mary's mother-in-law saw with envy how the jewels enhanced the peerless Queen-*dauphine* (such was her title) as she went her gracious and graceful way about the court at Fontainebleau. It was an ideal partnership of lovely woman and lovely pearls, and glamour as well as virtue passed into them from their wearer as she caressed them with those delicate fingers, 'fashioned and moulded so well that they were no less perfect than those of Aurora', as Brantôme declared when he watched them playing on the lute.

For the short space of fifteen months Catherine had to suffer the supremacy of this girl-wife who scornfully alluded to her as 'merchant's daughter'. Mary herself then rejoiced in threefold royalty as Queen of Scotland and France and of England, too, since Elizabeth was considered a mere bastard of Anne Boleyn. It was, however, only a brief and glorious episode in her life and when it ended with the death of her ailing young husband duty summoned her away from the delights of the French court to her unknown kingdom in the north, a call which she obeyed sadly and regretfully. With her the pearls came to Scotland, to remind the Queen of gayer scenes as she paced through the dances at Holyrood or sat in council with her stern and scheming nobles. How magnificent was her collection of these ornaments may be seen in the Leven and Melville portrait.

Too often the pearls must then have felt upon them the tears they are said to symbolize and over which John Knox gloated. So much was crowded into that small span of years: a little fugitive happiness, many plots, much treachery and inevitable tragedy. Roused by her marriage to the Earl of Bothwell the confederate lords became openly hostile and defeated Mary at Carberry Hill on the 15th of June 1567. On being sent as a prisoner to Lochleven Castle she begged the Earl of Moray, one of her father's numerous illegitimate offspring, to take care of the diamonds which she had bequeathed to the Crown and future Queens of Scotland and of her other jewels so as to preserve them for herself and her child, the little Prince James. We have seen how a half-brother had once given the pearls to

64

Mary's granddaughter, Elizabeth of Bohemia, painted by Mierevelt with the pearls bestowed as a wedding gift by her father

The pearls graced yet another royal beauty when Queen Alexandra wore them at the Coronation of 1901. *By Sir Luke Fildes, R.A.*

enrich a sister in her need, now in reverse Mary's scheming half-brother, although at first he pretended reluctance in agreeing to her request, took possession of her valuables in order to finance her enemies whose leader he was. Within a few months he had entered into negotiations with the Queen of England for their sale and on the 1st of May 1568 his secret messenger, Michael Elphinstone, was displaying the now famous *cordons* of pearls to Elizabeth and Leicester.

Meanwhile Catherine de Medici had got wind of the business and showed how eager she was to recover the pearls by sending an envoy, Bochetel de la Forest, to make an offer for them. He, however, was not allowed to see the pearls and had to content himself with reporting to the Queen Regent that the gossip of Whitehall was all of the unparalleled beauty of the six great ropes, strung like 'patenostres'.

Then came the dramatic news that Mary had escaped from Lochleven and was gathering an army of her loyal followers. The English Queen set about business in earnest while Elphinstone walked delicately among the rather unfriendly English and showed himself so 'debonaire' that no unpleasantness disturbed the negotiations between Elizabeth and Moray. London jewellers and Italian merchants were summoned to value the pearls, and on the 15th of May de la Forest had to inform Catherine that the coveted necklace had been sold to Elizabeth for £3,600. The Queen Regent of France had already written another letter begging him by all means in his power to obtain the pearls, but her envoy's report checked the dispatch of this order and Catherine, nobly or more probably hypocritically concealing her true feelings, substituted another letter bidding de la Forest trouble no more as she wished Elizabeth to have the pearls and would indeed have sent them to her if she had been lucky enough to get them!

Simultaneous with the sale of the coveted pearls came Mary's final defeat at Langside and on her arrival in England as a fugitive seeking Elizabeth's protection she learned of her half-brother's duplicity. She wrote at once to Lord Fleming imploring him to urge the King of France to forbid the sale of her jewels, but her friends in that country already knew that the English Queen had them in her possession, though they believed it was as a gift and not by purchase.

Only too soon did the unhappy Queen of Scots realize what treatment she might expect in England, and though she restrained herself from saying too much she wept bitterly at the rape of her treasures and wrote to Elizabeth beseeching her to stop the sale and declaring she would be 'content for her sister-queen to have them, since between Elizabeth and herself she made no difference'. It was natural for Mary to be shocked at the idea of such jewels falling into any hands that were not royal; they were not, as she said, 'meat fit for traitors'. But these 'stowte words' came too late and though Elizabeth warned Moray not to proceed with the sale of the Queen of Scots' diamonds he continued to dispose of much of her jewellery to finance his party, a profitable business for which the Scottish Parliament gave him a guarantee that 'it shall not hurt him hereafter'.

The rapid course of Mary's earlier years slowed down to the long-drawn-out period of imprisonment and when at last she went to her death on the scaffold Elizabeth must surely have felt a twinge of pity as she clasped the dead Queen's pearls round her neck. Then she, too, came to her end and the son of her rival and victim arrived from Scotland to reign in her place, bringing with him a Danish wife to fall heiress to the great Eliza's wardrobe and jewel-caskets. This Queen Anne, however, had her own extravagant taste in jewellery and adored colourful gems, so perhaps it was no sacrifice for her to see the ropes of pearls handed over once again to a royal bride when her daughter Elizabeth married Frederick, the Elector Palatine of the Rhine. These jewels that had known an Italian, French, Scottish and Danish mistress now found a fitting successor in Queen Mary's granddaughter, 'the Queen of Hearts' who inherited so much of her allure and who rode upon the storms of her chequered life with such gay gallantry. The tributes which were paid to her charm throughout her adventurous career began while she was still a child playing in her 'Fairy Farm' with her little friends tricked out as Arcadian shepherds and shepherdesses. 'Whatever was excellent and lofty in Queen Elizabeth,' wrote one courtier, 'is all compressed in the tender age of this virgin Princess. She has gentle manners, natural courtesy, and is of lovely beauty.' Her mother might sneer at the match she made and nickname her 'Goody Palgrave' but she must have been a radiant figure as the Londoners watched the sixteen-year-old bride and bridegroom in jewelled cloth of silver pass in procession along the outer gallery of Whitehall. It is true that Elizabeth on that day wore a golden crown with pendants of diamond and pearl shining in her fair curls, but her real coronation came later in St. Wenceslaus' Cathedral at Prague when she was acclaimed Queen of Bohemia —'the Winter Queen' who reigned for a year and a day and saw her new homeland ravaged with war. From England her father replied 'in sour ink' to her piteous appeals that he should help her husband, but Elizabeth was never to lack a devoted band of adherents who worshipped her beauty and bravery. Poets sang her praises and artists painted her, among them Van Mierevelt who portrayed her with the historic pearls twined in heavy ropes round her breast and waist. Of her numerous children Prince Rupert and Prince Maurice, those impetuous cavaliers who hastened to the support of their ill-fated Uncle Charles in England, were worthy sons of so dashing a mother, but it is Sophia, her twelfth child, who is of most interest to us. As wife of Ernest Augustus she became the Duchess of Hanover whose eldest son, George Louis, after an unpleasant *contretemps* with his wife over her lover Königsmarck, left her a life prisoner in the Castle of Ahlden and came to England to reign as George I. With him the pearls returned to share in the dubious splendours of such consorts as Caroline, Charlotte and Adelaide. They were now Crown Jewels, an official and rather humdrum status which dulled their romance.

Redemption came with the reign of Victoria, although it involved the pearls in a rather unpleasant family row. When, on the accession of the young Queen, Hanover separated from Great Britain, the Duke of Cumberland, Victoria's uncle, became King of Hanover and demanded that those Crown Jewels which had come to England with George I should be handed over to him. Among them were the ropes of pearl which Prince Albert said were the finest in Europe. Great anxiety was felt at Court over the matter and the Government resisted their surrender. Much wrangling followed until a Commission was appointed and, after a lengthy inquiry, was about to give its decision when one of its members, Chief Justice Tindal, died. The remaining two, Lord Lyndhurst and Lord Langdale, were divided in opinion, so no award was made. The dispute dragged on for twenty years when another Commission was named to investigate the claim, the result being a settlement in favour of Hanover. The Queen and Prince Consort were naturally 'desperately annoyed' at what they considered an unfair award and Albert asked Lord Clarendon if Parliament could not be approached with a view to making good the loss of the pearls which Victoria was very fond of wearing. With supreme tact Lord Clarendon negatived the suggestion, pointing out that it would be better not to press the question since the Queen's popularity 'was in great measure owing to her own judicious conduct and abstinence from that extravagance which had marked the reign of George IV; that nobody cared whether she was attired in fine pearls or diamonds, and would rather rejoice to see her without them than that she should wear them when they belonged to somebody else; or that substitutes were supplied by funds raised by taxation.' Luckily, however, it was finally proved that the 'Hanoverian Pearls' had originally gone from England when Princess Elizabeth married her Elector Palatine and so they remained 'to be vested as heirlooms for ever in the British Crown'. But the memory of this dispute had spoilt their attraction for Queen Victoria and thenceforth they were rarely seen in public until Queen Alexandra gave them pride of place among her jewels at the Coronation of 1901 and wore them almost constantly after that. How perfectly these historic jewels enhanced royal dignity can be seen in her portrait by Sir Luke Fildes and also in Sir William Llewellyn's painting of the late Queen Mary. So it came about that they graced the third Queen Elizabeth they had known, the present Queen Mother, a compatriot of the Queen of Scots who first brought this treasure to a land once famed for its native pearls and assured its safe keeping as a rightful legacy to future Queens.

I met Clarendon last night, talked about the Hanoverian jewel question, that the Queen and Prince were desperately annoyed at the award, which they thought unfair. The Prince asked Clarendon whether Parliament could not be applied to, to make good the jewels, which were the very ones the Queen had always worn, and that the dignity of the Crown required she should be properly furnished with such ornaments. Clarendon told him it was out of the question, that the Government could not make any such application to Parliament, and that it was far better for *them* [the Court] that it should not be done, that her popularity was in great measure owing to her own judicious conduct and abstinence from that extravagance which had marked the reign of George IV, that nobody cared whether she was attired in fine pearls or diamonds, and would rather see her without them than that she should wear them when they belonged to somebody else, or that substitutes were supplied by funds raised by taxation. So they gave it up, as he says they are always ready to do when a matter is fairly put before them.

The Greville Diary

1568: 21 mita—Paris.

La Royne mere a M. de la Forest. Quant aulx bagues de la Royne d'Escosse, dont je vous ay escript dernierement, et desquelles la Royne d'Angleterre a retenu les perles, comme vous m'avez despuis mande, il n'est plus besoing de vous en mectre en poyne, pour ce que je desire qu'elle les retienne toutes, comme il est bien raisonnable; et, si je les avoiz, je les luy envoierois.

[The Queen-Mother to M. de la Forest. As to the jewels of the Queen of Scotland concerning which I recently wrote to you and from which the Queen of England has kept the pearls, there is no more need to trouble, for I wish her to keep them all, as is very reasonable; and if I had them, I should send them to her.]

The dispute about their ownership always rankled with Queen Victoria and was the chief reason why she seldom wore them, and when she did it was chiefly as a delicate hint to visiting potentates of the power and glory of the British monarchy.

One such occasion her Majesty noted in her diary. 'I dressed in a smart morning dress with my large pearls,' she wrote apropos of the visit to Windsor of the Shah Nasser-el-Din of Persia.

And evidently that eastern ruler was duly impressed. Indeed his eyes were seemingly so rivetted on the pearls while he was slipping the ribbon of a Persian Order over her Britannic Majesty's head and shoulders, that he knocked the royal lady's cap askew. 'But', recorded the royal diarist, 'the Grand Vizier came to the rescue.'

Queen Alexandra was stepping into the State Coach to go with the King to Westminster for the State Opening of Parliament when the pearls caught in the woodwork, a string broke, and scatter went scores of gems, mostly between coach wheels and horses' hoofs. And were not royal horses the well-trained animals they are, some of the Hanoverian pearls might, like Cleopatra's, have been crushed to powder, though in a very different cause. As it was, they were all safely collected, but not without much loss of dignity on the part of those royal footmen who had to grovel in quest of the rolling gems.

Mary Abbott: *Jewels of Romance and Renown*

AN ORKNEY CHILDHOOD

by F. Marian McNeill

By a happy freak of fortune my childhood was spent in the eighteenth century and my adolescence in the Edwardian era. I did not entirely bypass good Queen Victoria's golden reign, it is true, for we had only to drive a few miles from our rural parish to Kirkwall, the island capital, to enter it; but our roots were in the old, primitive Orkney that lay on the edge of the world—and the otherworld: the first inhabited by crofters, farmers, and fishermen—sensible, kindly, hard-working folk who instinctively put human values far above commercial ones, and whose way of life was co-operative, not competitive as in the world I was later to enter; the second inhabited by *trows* (trolls) and *fairocks* (fairies), witches and mermaids, who were none the less real because (witches apart) they were seldom, if ever, seen.

Although separated from the old life by two world wars, we still speak of the Manse as home, for there my father spent the whole of his long ministry; thither he brought his young bride; there we were all born and, in our early years, bred; and in later years we looked forward eagerly to our home-comings from school and University and from wanderings in all the airts.

Holm (pronounced Ham) is one of the pleasantest and most fertile parishes in Orkney. The Manse—a plain, rectangular, white-harled, blue-slated building—stood high on a southern slope. During the long dark winters it was harried by every gale that swept down from the Arctic, and for days at a stretch we would look out on a bare, treeless landscape, the blurred outline of rocks, leaden seas, and the ceaseless downpour of rain. But on the advent of spring, what a transformation!

71

There could hardly have been a lovelier prospect in the whole archipelago than that which our windows framed. To the south, the sea was studded with low green islands—Lambholm, Glimsholm, Hunda, Burray, South Ronaldshay and the rest; beyond them, separated by the silver streak of the Pentland Firth, lay the cliffs of Caithness, and, faintly blue on the horizon, the outline of Morven and the Sutherland hills, whilst in the west rose the mountainous island of Hoy, whose contours nightly showed purple-black against a blaze of crimson and gold.

Dominated by a great arch of sky, surrounded by wide seas, and looking out to far horizons (to whose lure we were later to succumb), we could not but be awed by the sense of illimitable space. Sometimes, driving home on a frosty night when the stars glittered overhead, my father would point out to us the planets and constellations, and it gave us a queer, uncanny thrill to realize that the earth could be at once so big and so small—so small in relation to the wide-flung map of the heavens, and so big in relation to the island we lived on, though that seemed big enough when we forgot (as we normally did) to look beyond it.

The motto of country ministers a generation or more ago seems to have been 'Blessed is he that hath his quiver full,' and my home, like many another Scottish manse, was furnished mainly with books and bairns. To feed his ever-growing family, my father farmed twenty acres that grew oats for the porridge-pot and the girdle and vegetables for the kail-pot; and he kept a few beasts and birds that supplied us with milk and butter and eggs, as well as wool for blankets and tweeds. Then there was a gig for trips on land and a dinghy for trips on the sea. A grand life for children!

Where money is scarce, rigid economy is necessary, but, in the true Scottish tradition, there were two things on which there was no economizing—hospitality and education. In summer the old Manse overflowed with young life, and apart from invited guests one never knew who the winds might blow in—an Oxford don or a packman. My father was by nature lavish, but with my mother's wise guidance the necessary economies were practised to swell the fund for our education. In our early years, we attended the excellent parish school, but meanwhile my mother, subordinating her social and intellectual gifts, patched and mended and made down garments, and denied herself in all sorts of ways, in order to send her daughters (after high school) to schools on the Continent (which after all cost no more, fares apart, than schools in Edinburgh or Glasgow), and, if they so wished, to accompany their brothers to the university she herself had longed for, but, being in advance of her times, had been denied.

On a fine summer day, how good it was to lie on the grass all starred with daisies and buttercups and watch the snow-white clouds drifting across the sky and forming themselves into ever-changing pictures, or to meander through meadows filled with dewy clover round which the bees hummed! Then beneath those wonderful windows of ours my father had dug a garden out of the heather. It was at its loveliest in the late spring, with masses of blue and white hyacinths, yellow daffodils and pheasant's eye narcissus. Later came tulips and roses—the little white cottage roses that smell so sweet—tall, flame-red 'pokers', blue columbine, and crimson peonies—a riot of colour framed by the garden railing, with the green fields and the blue sea beyond. The heather, that grew unmolested round the white-harled kirk beside us, would still come creeping up to the garden wall and enter surreptitiously by the little side gate, as if loath to abandon its ancient demesne. In the garden, too, stood a flagstaff that had been the mast, and a greenhouse that had been the deck-cabin of a schooner wrecked, years before, on the rocks of Rose Ness, a mile or two away. On those rocks I had many a time watched the great Atlantic breakers churn to foam, but now, in summer, their clamour had died down to a murmur. The sea before our windows was blue and green and purple, and brown-sailed fishing-boats passed up and down the sound. Owld Jock would climb the long loan from the village with his creel of silver herring, and Beenie, who presided in the kitchen, would run down to the gate for an ashetful and serve them up for supper all frizzling in their golden coats of oatmeal.

Then the van, a miniature shop on wheels, would lumber along the road, and we smaller children would run down to the garden gate at Beenie's heels and wait eagerly until her big basket was filled with loaves and cookies and sundry mysterious packages; for the vanman never failed to reach down a big glass jar, and, with a 'Ha'e, bairns!', fill our small outstretched hands with gaily coloured fruit drops that sparkled in the sun and tasted just as good as they looked.

Tea with one or other of our little school-friends was a special treat. I can still recall vividly the moorland path leading to a certain snug little croft, the clumps of foxgloves and purple thistles, the scent of heather and bog myrtle, the singing of the hill birds, the sparkling of the sun on the distant sea, the barking of the collie, the warm greeting at the door, the pungent odour of peats burning on the wide, open hearth, the delectable nutty smell of oatcakes toasting on the girdle, the singing of the kettle, the straw-backed Orkney chairs, the home-made wooden creepies, the table spread with homely cottage fare. All this had a charm for me that was lacking in the Kirkwall drawing-rooms with their Victorian furniture, in spite of their superior tea-table delicacies, for which I had always an appreciative palate.

Then the lovely midsummer nights when the gloaming

merged into the dawn! Bed was a hateful word. The air was so still that you could hear the lowing of the kye as they returned from pasture, the barking of a dog, or the whistling of a herdie-lad across the sound in Burray. Along the road old Magnus, his day's work done, would sit on a creepie at his cottage door, playing the melodeon, and the lads and lasses, laughing and chattering, would pass by in small bands—never mixed, for Orcadian ideas of propriety did not then permit even the semblance of wooing save under cover of dusk.

On a fine moonlight evening my big brothers would take us younger children out in the boat and sail round to Rose Ness, where we would row into the cool green depths of one of the great bird-haunted caves; then, moving further out, we would try to lure the seals with song or flute to follow the boat. Sometimes we would spend cold but exciting hours far out at sea, fishing for sillocks (saithe in their first season). We would 'dite' our catch in a moonlit rock pool; then, home at cock-crow, we would coax the kitchen fire to life and proceed to cook our catch, dipping each tiny, headless fish into seasoned oatmeal and popping it into a pan of hot butter; then, while they spluttered and browned, we made tea and buttered some fresh barley bannocks; and thus we feasted while the rest of the household slept.

After summer came the dowie days of harvest, and soon we were in the chill embrace of the northern winter. Day after day we would batter our way through the wind and rain to school. Breakfast and tea were served in lamplight, and in the long dark evenings fearful shadows lurked in every corner—or were they, as I sometimes suspected, not shadows, but the uncanny creatures of the otherworld? Yet winter, too, had its joys. Shut off from the outer world by raging winds and seas, we lived largely in a world of fancy, inspired by song and story. Fairy tales from Hans Andersen and Grimm, stories from the Greek, Celtic and Norse mythologies, the Waverley novels, the Border ballads, the exploits of Wallace and Bruce, the tragedy of Mary Stuart, the tales of the Covenanters, the adventures of Prince Charlie, the achievements of the great missionaries and explorers—all these were woven for us into a multi-coloured tapestry. Then the family recreation was music—piano, fiddle and flute, and, not least, song. There were my father's haunting

Gaelic songs, my mother's Scottish folk-songs and Victorian song albums, and much else. Later there were added to our store of music the volumes of Bach, Beethoven and Mozart, of Schubert, Schumann and Brahms, that my elder sisters brought back from their schools in Germany and Switzerland—an abundant reward for my parents' economies. My father, lively, choleric and affectionate, fiddled and sang and had a fund of funny stories; and my mother, more austere in temperament, but wise and tolerant, had tastes more cultivated than was usual in an obscure country manse. So our life, though poor in material things, was rich in other respects.

In childhood we take our parents for granted, and too often it is not until after we have lost them that we fully realise what they meant to us. In my own home we acquired, almost unconsciously, an awareness of 'the eternal verities' and a respect for human personality that transcended all distinctions of race, class and creed. We learned, too—most useful to a family like ours, that money runs away from!—that the very best things in life cost little or nothing, provided one is able to enjoy good books, good talk, good music, good pictures, friendship and neighbourliness, and the beauty and wonder of nature.

A few years ago I revisited Orkney, and on my way home from a round of visits in the parish stopped at the lonely churchyard down by the sea. Among the surf-washed tombstones I found that beneath which the bodies of my parents lie. Other names had been added to it, though the family graves are scattered far and wide. Dusk was gathering as I lingered there, and I reflected that as a child I should have been terrified to be alone at that hour in such a place. But now I felt no fear at all, not even grief, but only gratitude for all I owed my parents and my home. I came away feeling curiously serene. Why? Because I simply don't believe there is such a thing as death!

⁂ ⁂ ⁂ ⁂ ⁂ ⁂ ⁂ ⁂ ⁂ ⁂ ⁂ ⁂ ⁂ ⁂ ⁂ ⁂

Orkney and Shetland are separate counties and proud of it. They are the clusters which map-makers habitually tuck into a square frame in the Moray Firth. Whether because of the dubious proximity to Scotland, or the off-hand disposal, this position on the atlas angers the Norse-tending inhabitants, as I found in reverse once on receiving many letters commending a lucky editorial decision to publish a newspaper map which showed the islands in their true place, trailing off towards Norway. Orkney and Shetland were Viking ruled, and to some extent Viking peopled, in a diminishing way from the end of the ninth century until the marriage of James III to Princess Margaret of the Norse in 1469, when they were handed over as a pledge of the Princess's dowry, which is still unpaid. Although they had by that time long since returned to the Scottish sphere of influence, the modern attitude of the Orcadian or Shetlander to Scotland is a kind of reminiscent twinkle, as much as to show that Scandinavia may pay up any day and take them back where they belong.

Alastair M. Dunnett
The Highlands and Islands of Scotland

CHILDHOOD

Long time he lay upon the sunny hill,
  To his father's house below securely bound.
Far off the silent, changing sound was still,
  With the black islands lying thick around.

He saw each separate height, each vaguer hue,
  Where the massed islands rolled in mist away,
And though all ran together in his view
  He knew that unseen straits between them lay.

Often he wondered what new shores were there.
  In thought he saw the still light on the sand,
The shallow water clear in tranquil air,
  And walked through it in joy from strand to strand.

Over the sound a ship so slow would pass
  That in the black hill's gloom it seemed to lie.
The evening sound was smooth like sunken glass,
  And time seemed finished ere the ship passed by.

Grey tiny rocks slept round him where he lay,
  Moveless as they, more still as evening came,
The grasses threw straight shadows far away,
  And from the house his mother called his name.

Edwin Muir

ORKNEY

God, Who in days of old
  Created the sea
And the skies—O there behold
  What beauties be—
These treeless islands set
  Where the wild goose flies,
Lest men should e'er forget
  The sea and the skies.

from *Country Sonnets and Other Poems* by Robert Rendall

THE SCOTTISH STUDENT TODAY

by Douglas Young

WE have more Scottish students now than ever, and drawn from a wider variety of types. To get an idea of *the* Scottish student is about as difficult as glimpsing the Loch Ness Monster, or one hump of one of that breed.

For centuries the *praefervidum ingenium Scotorum*, the Scots' unco het ingyne, has been addicted to learning and disputation, in Gaelic and other tongues, as they came into fashion. We hear of Joannes Scotus Erigena, in the ninth century—a Scot born in Eire, or as some claim in Ayr, and perhaps an Ulster Scot, dining tête-à-tête with Charles the Bald of France: when the King pawkily asked, after some bouts of wine-bibbing, *'Quid distat inter Scotum et sottum?'*, 'What separates a Scot from a sot?', to which John the Scot promptly replied, *'Mensa tantum'*, 'Only a table.'

Already before the Wallace and Bruce wars we find Scots in leading places among the European intelligentzia, the Franciscan John Duns Scotus being so denigrated by less enterprising thinkers that his name came to signify a *dunce*, while Dante consigned to a low circle of his Inferno the eminent Aristotelian scholar Michael Scott, 'the Wizard', with whom he differed on international politics.

A Scots lady, Devorguilla, founded Balliol College at Oxford, still a resort of lads o pairts; and a nationalist Bishop of Moray founded bursaries for a Scots College at Paris; while many Scots stravaiged as far as Bologna or Padua for their learning. Universities are by their very nature international institutions, and most northern European nations were content to send their sons southward, to Paris or Italy, till well on in the fifteenth or even the sixteenth century. Scotland was indeed comparatively early in securing a university on her own soil, when Bishop Wardlaw of St. Andrews obtained Bulls from Pope Benedict XIII. He was one of three Popes simultaneously claiming the tiara, and had few supporters outside Aragon: so that the canny Bishop may have got the needful Papal documents on the cheap —a sort of scrub Bull. St. Andrews started in 1411, and a generation later the Bishop of Glasgow thought he had better have a university too; and before the fifteenth century was out the Bishop of Aberdeen had induced James IV to endow King's College. After the Reformation of 1560 James VI erected Edinburgh, somewhat on the model of Calvin's Geneva, as 'the Toun's College', and a great Protestant magnate founded Marischal College at New Aberdeen. So that Scotland could boast five universities two hundred and fifty years before England had her third. In Victorian times King's and Marischal were merged.

But all these universities were small, hardly more than equivalent to colleges at Oxford or Cambridge. They fostered occasional talents of the brightest order, like John Napier of Merchiston; the Gregory breed of mathematicians; George Buchanan the historian and poet, than whom no writer ever had a greater command of both prose and verse in Latin; the philosophers Hutcheson and Reid; Adam Smith the economist; Joseph Black the physicist; Lord Kelvin, and so on. From the later eighteenth century Edinburgh and Glasgow began to grow in numbers and fame, and to attract many from outside Scotland. Nonconformists from England, Wales, and Ireland, came to Scotland, the English universities being Anglican. Dr Helen Waddell, the authority on the medieval wandering scholars, tells how her Ulster forebears landed at Stranraer and walked to college in Glasgow, finding milk and oatcakes laid out by the kindly farmers *en route*. Edinburgh was for two generations Europe's chief intellectual centre after Paris.

Apart from their interesting traditions, often matters for pride, the four Scottish universities have marked local personalities. Oxford on its ford, Cambridge at its bridge, owe their establishment to being focal points of communication; but are themselves rather dull and dreary in site and environment. St. Andrews has in the highest degree been endowed by the *genius loci,* on its bold bluff above the North Sea, with the ruins of archiepiscopal magnificence; while that half of the university which thrives in Dundee has an admirable academic precinct in one of the finest city-sites in Europe. Edinburgh has buildings worthy of that city 'carved of mountain and romance', as the poet Lewis Spence called it. Aberdeen has varied charm and dignity poised in granite between its diverse estuaries. Glasgow has unfortunately suffered destruction of its renaissance abode in what was a charming little city till the industrial revolution; but there is a certain grandeur in the Victorian Gothic that crowns the Gilmorehill, and looks down on Clydeside's tenements and cranes with the pride of a Norman knight bringing efficiency and order to a backward tribal peasantry.

These local personalities imponderably but undoubtedly mould the sensibilities of those who resort to them for learning. But who are these? And how many? And why do they come? How do they live? Largest is Glasgow, with (as I write) nearly 5,000 full-time students; then Edinburgh, with about 4,500; while Aberdeen and St. Andrews (with Dundee) each have around 1,700. At each place the majority are of Scottish domicile, with probably the largest proportion at Aberdeen, which is so firmly rooted into the north-east, tapping also part of the Highlands and the Orkneys and Shetland, as Dee and Don drain their mountain-fringed straths. But many come from the Scottish diaspora in England, offspring of the export surplus of medicine-men and heids o depairtments, business executives and engineers. Others come from the Dominions and Colonies. Not long ago at St. Andrews I heard a lecture by an eminent Jewish savant on the Arabic poetry of Spain, when most of the discussion was carried on by negroes from West and East Africa. The former Principal of Aberdeen was active in fostering a West African University, while the late Principal of St. Andrews performed a similar service in the West Indies. Pakistan and Egypt send students to learn engineering or medicine. American post-graduates come for theology or all sorts of things, including just 'European culture' in general. I came across a Persian and a Salonika Greek and a Spaniard researching in law at Queen's College, Dundee. There are all sorts of people, as is right in an international institution. And of course quantities of English, Welsh, and Irish students and staff-teachers, not to mention Poles and German Jews.

Why do they come? Chiefly, of course, as always, to take courses qualifying for a profession, such as law or medicine or teaching, or enabling them to pass an examination for the Civil Service. But also, one hopes, for the old ideal of a liberal education. How do they live? At Glasgow and Edinburgh very many live at home and commute daily, like typists or bank-clerks, from Kilmarnock or Dumbarton, Peebles or Kirkcaldy. It is commonly agreed that many of such commuters miss a good deal of the unassessable but certain advantages of university life, which cannot flow in its richest abundance inside classrooms. Many live in lodgings, 'bunks', some of which have ancient traditions and idiosyncrasies of their own, extending over the lives of generations of students and landladies, 'bunkwives'. But I fear the old 'bunk' life is dwindling. Through the growth of non-academic tourism it is certainly weaker in St. Andrews than it was when I wore the old red gown; and it is weaker than I have found it in Leiden or Uppsala. Maybe in Aberdeen there is a richer symbiosis of Town and Gown, through the student-landlady nexus, than elsewhere.

St. Andrews has led the way in residential education, such as Robert Fergusson the poet had in the eighteenth century, or Andrew Lang in the nineteenth; and has for nearly seventy years now pioneered particularly in facilities for women. But Edinburgh and the rest are developing rapidly their systems of hostels. Attempts are also being made, again led by St. Andrews, to cultivate closer informal relations between students and staff; for the transmission of culture and of intellectual attitudes is best accomplished not merely by injection in laboratories and lecture-halls but by the infection of personal contacts.

Scotland has an old tradition of the poor student, struggling along on pokes of meal and bursaries; and also of the frivolous dilettante, the 'chronic', like James Bridie in Edwardian days, or Eric Linklater's characters in *White-maa's Saga*. The academic guillotines cut off the chronics untimely nowadays; but a certain amount of financial stringency still affects many, or most, students. Scottish awards from public sources are much less than those in England, and those are found inadequate. Students have to waste too much time in vacations earning cash at dull jobs, when they should be cultivating their individual talents for the good of society.

The cult of marks, of examination passes, is perhaps too devoutly pursued by some, too lightly spurned by others—including myself in my young days. Our students could benefit, I believe, from rather more extra-curricular activities directed to general culture, as Dr T. J. Honeyman pointed out in his rectorial address, stressing the need to cultivate the emotions and imagination. In stimulating taste and a variety of social and political interests, the international elements help the blate-blooming native Scots. Largely to an enlightened Englishman, Sir Edward Appleton, is due the belated, and hesitant, cultivation of Scottish studies. Without national salt the international broth will be gey wersh.

EDINBURGH, 14 *February* 1666.

It being informed be Andrew Cheyn Thesaurer of the Colledge that the present Janitor had at his owen hand struck through twa ston walls for brewing of drink That he at his own hand without acquainting the Thesaurer repaired severall things in the Colledge and put up exorbitant accomptis And that he had not made payment of the chamber maills tho he had uplifted the same And that he had assisted the stealing of goodis in over the Toun Wallis And being challenged for breaking through the wall he answered that baillie Drummond former thesaurer had given him allowance who utterlie denyed the same Besyde his gameing and playing at the lotterie The Counsell appoynts the Thesaurer of the Colledge to cause wairne the janitor to compear befor the Counsell on Fryday nixt.

The Burgh Records of Edinburgh

83

Her morn again, her skies, her happy glowing
   Of mind and body. Youth and high heart are home
To take the wine of all the dayspring flowing
   From dawnlight and from foam.
Gulls for her standards o'er a young town streaming,
   Wind-laved towers musicked anew from sea,
And in the blue-white air of morning gleaming
   Her deathless bejantry.

> *Mary the Queen still in 'The Purpose' dances.*
>   *James Melvill's spinet plays.*
> *No Assynt shadow falls upon the Marquis*
>   *Riding the Kinkell braes.*
> *No Mantuan knife is hungry yet for Crichton,*
>   *No fire for Hamilton.*
> *And half a nation's story now as bejants*
>   *All to the golf are gone.*
> *Murray is writing in a room off North Street,*
>   *Lang's in the Library.*
> *No grave for these we loved is dug in Flanders.*
>   *They all are here today.*

from 'Kate Kennedy—Her Day, A St. Andrews Bardic Ode'
from *The Old Stalker and Other Verses* by J. B. Salmond

84

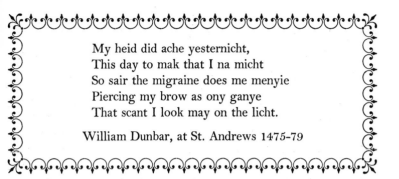

My heid did ache yesternicht,
This day to mak that I na micht
So sair the migraine does me menyie
Piercing my brow as ony ganye
That scant I look may on the licht.

William Dunbar, at St. Andrews 1475-79

It was by no means uncommon for students at Scottish Universities to live at College on as little as Dewar did.* In the evidence led before the Royal Commission of 1826, it is stated that the cost was frequently as low as £15 a session, including fees, and was in some cases even less. Breakfast on porridge and milk; for dinner, some days broth and a little meat, other days, bread and milk or potatoes and herring, or potatoes and a little butter; tea in the afternoon or evening; no supper. Some students had no fire in their rooms, and others little or no candlelight. A former St. Andrew student gives similar evidence before the Commissioners. One student of St. Andrews twenty years after Dewar's day, whom I had the pleasure of knowing, told me that all he spent on his food was one shilling and twopence for a week or a fortnight—I do not remember which. I asked, How was that? He replied 'When I came to college I brought from home a sack of peasemeal. I had peasemeal brose for breakfast, peasemeal brose for dinner, and peasemeal brose for supper, and the outlay of 1/2 was for milk with which to eat the brose.' He added that the student who lived above him was even more economical. He came from Dundee; his mother was a washerwoman. With him he brought a sack of potatoes and a large fat ham. For dinner he handed to his landlady three or four potatoes to boil, with instructions not to peel them, and they, with a slice of ham, formed his dinner. From his walk along the sands he brought in enough driftwood to keep his fire going.

* This student's total expenditure for seven sessions was £101.

from *Duncan Dewar's Accounts*, 1819-27

85

Much Honoured,

On Thursday last at night a student in the Old Colledge went to St Leonard's Colledge to see an acquaintance of his there who had provided 4 ounces of pouder at least to be spent in squibs on the friday, quiich they began to prepare that night, but as they lookt carelessly to themselves or while one of them would forsooth try the first squib, they kindled all the pouder that lay spread on the table; quhereby the right hand and whole face of the one was blasted, & the cheeks and both the hands of the other: they are both under the Chirurgian's cure, and tho the present smart of the burning be very painful, yet it's expected they may both recover without any blemish on their faces. This being the first news K: and T: told me on friday's morning as they returned from Prayers made me very apprehensive for them that day for Tum tua res agitur paries cum proximus ardet: and seeing that was a playday [Queen Anne's birthday] upon the accompt of the solemnities thereof I did not suffer them to go out before dinner, and being importuned to allow them to see the several Colours of the Town, I went out with them about 3 a clock and after I had brought them back, I did not so much as let them go out to Evening prayers in the Colledge that night for fear they might have sustained some harm at the bonefires, quhereat some were discharging Pistols & others throwing coals at one another.

James Morice, a tutor at St. Andrews

THE REAL
HUMOUR OF SCOTLAND

by Mary Fleming

To the outer world the most typical Scots joke is summed up
in the hoary cry 'Bang went saxpence!' *Punch* fathered this
classic jest during the eighteen-sixties, as the complaint of a
thrifty Scot in London, but in doing so it was merely giving
body to a jest that had been in the air for centuries, probably
since a host of poor but proud northerners followed James VI
and I to London on the Union of the Crowns. Certainly the
notion is still good for a laugh anywhere south of Berwick, and
turns up like a much worn bawbee every time a Scots character
is brought into a play or film. When it has looked like going
out of currency, certain Scots comedians and joke writers have
given it a burnish and sent it spinning round once more, despite
the fact that the real Scottish humour is a very much more
precious coin—rich gold as against the most debased metal.
So lives on the comic Scot of popular fiction, red-nosed, kilted,
leaning on a crooked stick, and grasping a purse tenanted by
moths and the smallest of small change.

Fortunately we have for home consumption a fund of humour
which the incomer could hardly be expected to appreciate, so
bound up is it with language and psychological differences.
Sydney Smith declared that it required a surgical operation to
get a joke into a Scotsman's head. To which one might reply
that nothing short of a century's domicile in Scotland could
begin to convey to the Sassenach the nuances of Scots humour.
We are in some ways the original poker-faced comedians, let-
ting our jokes escape reluctantly from half closed lips, and
looking at the hearer with slanted eyes to see if he is quick

enough to appreciate the point. Add to this technique the vast differences in syntax, dialect and pronunciation, and one could hardly expect the Southerner to understand our more characteristic jokes.

Indeed those which rely on the expressiveness of the Scots language may even be lost on a generation of young Scots more or less ignorant of the old tongue, but to those of us who absorbed it in childhood certain words carry an irresistible if untranslatable sense of fun. There is, for instance, the tale of the man who had listened long and patiently to a friend, extolling the inner virtues of his new but plain wife. 'Man, Jamie,' he said when he could get a word in, 'it's a peety ye couldna flype her.'

Quick also with the Scots *mot juste* was the old woman who was being patronized by a superior person who wanted to know why she did not like a certain preacher. 'Perhaps he is too deep for you?' the visitor inquired. 'Na, na,' was the swift reply, 'he's no ower deep, but he's *drumly!*'

The quiet retort, typical of a reticent folk, does not however always rely on the Scots language, but springs from a native wit that only becomes apparent after some acquaintance with Scotland. Again a delightful example comes from the lips of an elderly woman, this time a wifie wearied by the importunities of a boastful packman. 'Whaur d'ye come frae?' she asked. 'The Border', said he. 'I thocht sae,' was the dry rejoinder, 'for we aye think the selvedge the weakest part o the web.'

It is language, once again, plus a comic alliterativeness, which makes Dean Ramsay's favourite joke still as funny as when it was first set down. For readers who may not know this ripest of Scots chestnuts, the Laird of Balnamoon was being driven home by his servant Harry after a convivial evening with a fellow laird. He had been given cherry brandy in mistake for port, and as a result was in a state of owlish dignity. As they came to the most solitary part of their moorland road the laird's hat and wig blew away and Harry had to stop and retrieve them. Balnamoon took his hat graciously, but with drunken capriciousness jibbed at the wig. 'It's no my wig, Hairy, lad; it's no my wig.' Quite at the end of his patience, and wearying to get home, Harry remonstrated with his master: 'Ye'd best tak it sir, for there's nae *waile* [choice] o wigs on Munrimmon Muir!'

88

Eighteenth century Edinburgh, with its galaxy of wits among the professional and aristocratic classes, provided a host of stories which though typically Scots were yet of wider appeal, as befitted men who had many contacts with the greater world. But some of them were homely enough, as when the Hon. Henry Erskine congratulated a very thin friend who was eating a dried haddock on 'looking so like his meat'. The same Henry, however, could have been comprehended quite well in London's West End, when he refused the loan of a silk gown from the retiring Lord Advocate on his own appointment to that office. 'Never shall it be said', he quipped, 'that Henry Erskine adopted the *abandoned habits* of his predecessor.'

Sometimes legal circles yielded grim jests indeed, but then the Scot has always treated death and the Devil with a certain hardy familiarity. From the aftermath of the seventeenth century's religious troubles comes the famous retort made by Gilbert Elliot to his friend Covenanting William Veitch, whose cause he had successfully pleaded as an advocate. The former advocate was by this time a judge, and on meeting him Veitch had said: 'Aye Gibbie, had it no been for me, ye'd still be writing papers at a plack a page.' The reply was properly crushing: 'Aye, and had it no been for me, Willie, the pyets [magpies] wad hae pykit yer pate on the Netherbow Port.'

This ability to look Death in the eye and extract some humour from its terrors is characteristic of many Scots stories, and often is allied with a sense of the fantastic which comes from deep racial springs. Death might be a sinister figure with a scythe who, as Burns says, 'spak richt howe', but our ancestors could answer his summons or thole his nearness with a macabre jest. There is to illustrate this the wonderful anecdote of an ancient lady, Miss Johnstone of Westerhill, who lay dying on a night of terrible storm. Those about her bed saw her lips move, and bent closer to hear her last words. Faintly but indomitably she was heard to say: 'Eh, sirs, what a nicht for me to be fleein' thro' the air!'

Another story, much enjoyed by an older generation of Scots, told how a certain laird took his leave of life. He was present at one of the great convivial gatherings of the eighteenth century, when one of his neighbours thought he looked strange. 'What gars Garscadden luik sae gash?' he speired of the man sitting on his other side. 'Och, Garscadden's been wi' his Maker these twa oors,' was the easy reply. 'I saw him step awa, but I didna like to disturb the good company.'

On a different social level comes another example of the same hardy spirit. Death might swoop, but it was an inevitable visitation and the decencies of everyday life must be observed. So evidently thought the old dame who bent over her dying husband with the query: 'Wullie, Wullie, as lang's ye can speak, are ye for your funeral baps roond or square?'

In a country always strongly imbued with the democratic spirit many of the stories treat of the relationship between employer and employed. There was little of the 'God bless the squire and his relations' attitude north of the Tweed. The stubbornly individual Scot very rightly spoke his mind when he felt the need to do so, but allied with his outspokenness was a sense of loyalty to his master which gave him, he thought, a right to speak as one of the family. The most classic example of this relates of the exasperated gentleman who told his servant that he would have to go. 'I'll no gang,' said the domestic tyrant firmly. 'If ye dinna ken when ye've got a guid servant, I ken when I've got a guid maister.' Another of these worthies was met with by a lady staying as a guest in a big house. While she was there, outside guests were asked to dine. During the meal she signalled to the manservant that she would like another potato. At first he ignored the summons, but when it was repeated came quite close and whispered loudly: 'There's juist twa in the dish, and they maun be keepit for the strangers.'

Sometimes these characters treated their superiors as if they were fractious children, like the beadle who thought his master over fussy when he came in drenched with rain just before the service. The minister, who was a noted bore in the pulpit, kept on exclaiming: 'I'm awfu' weet, I'm awfu' weet,' to which at last his irritated servitor retorted: 'Ye'd best gang up to the poopit, ye'll be dry eneuch there!'

They could, however, be a tower of strength in difficulties, as a certain minister discovered when snowed up in a remote Highland parish. His supply of snuff had run out, and he could not get his sermon down on paper without the help of his accustomed pinch. He confided his desperate state to the

90

church officer who with a sudden cry of 'Hae!' disappeared into
the kirk. Soon he was back, bearing a brimming snuff-mull.
'Where did you get it?' his astonished master inquired. 'Och,'
was the pawky reply, 'I juist soopit the poopit!'

There were funny stories relating to the naïevté of country
Scots, like that about the man-servant bidden to 'carry (i.e.
convey) the ladies to the drawing-room' who did so literally,
remarking to one left behind, 'Bide ye there till I come for
ye!' But on the whole the pith of Scots humour consists of
awareness and a nice sense of phrasing. Even the 'naitrels'
could be consciously funny, like the Laird of Udny's fool. His
master was debating what to plant on a certain field, when
Jamie Fleeman gave utterance. 'Plant it wi' factors, Laird,'
he chuckled, 'they thrive in every place; tho' deil curse it,
they're no a very profitable crop!'

These stories are, of course, merely the *hors-d'œuvres* to the
feast of Scots humour, a feast which includes the inimitable
characters of Scott, the sly fun of certain ballads like 'Get Up
and Bar the Door,' or the daft exuberance of Burns in gay

mood. In a few lines from the song 'Last May a Braw Wooer' he etches a laughable pen portrait of a lassie baiting a fickle swain who has temporarily transferred his attentions to her cousin, and now wants to be taken back:

> I speired for my cousin fu' couthy and sweet,
>   Gin she had recovered her hearin',
> And how her new shoon fit her auld shachled feet,
>   By, heavens! how he fell a-swearin', a-swearin',
>   By heavens, how he fell a-swearin'!

Scott can draw from the spectacle of the mother-ridden Cuddy Headrigg in Covenanting times a picture of wry despair, and a wealth of typically native remonstrance that is now a classic of its kind: 'The foul fa' ye, that I suld sae sae . . . for a lang-tongued, clavering wife, as my faither, honest man, aye ca'd ye. Couldna ye let the leddy alane wi' your whiggery? . . . This is a waur dirdum than we got frae Mr Gudyill when he garr'd me refuse to eat the plum-porridge on Yule-eve, as if it were ony matter to God or man whether a ploughman had suppit on minched pies or sour sowens.'

Then there are those Caledonian inspired idiocies by David Rorie. 'The Lum Hat Wantin' a Croon', and 'The Pawky Duke'. The latter, to some extent, tips its balmoral bonnet towards the English idea of the comic Scot, but does it with such a neatness of rhythm and amusing use of Scots, that only the humourless will reject such lively nonsense verse:

> There aince was a very pawky duke,
>   Far kent for his joukery-pawkery,
> Wha owned a hoose wi' a gran' outlook,
>   A gairden an' a rockery.
>
> *Chorus*
>
> Hech, mon, the pawky duke,
> Hoot-aye an' a rockery,
> For a bonnet-laird wi' a sma' kail-yaird
> Is naething but a mockery.

In 'The Lum Hat Wantin' a Croon', there is one verse which could only have come out of the Scottish luckybag, with its nippy use of the retort discourteous. Readers will recall that an old woman, trying to salvage food and faring from the sea, is carried away in the flood in strange company. The fisher who spies her exclaims aloud:

—'It's a man overboord,' cries he,
'Ye leear,' says she, 'I'll droon!
A man on a boord, it's a wife on a gate,
It's auld Mistress Mackintosh here wi' a skate,
And a lum hat wantin' the croon!'

Is typical Scots humour dying out? Have our humorists nothing to fall back on but kitchen comedy and the loud-voiced jests of the industrial areas? Not entirely, one would imagine, since there is still a large rural population, using the old tongue in comparative purity, expressing itself with the characteristic pithiness of the Scot. Not so long as professional men in our country—doctors, lawyers, ministers—note and cherish the examples which come within their ken. Even our dramatists have moved away from the kitchen and the kailyaird, seeking to strike a new vein in the humorous fantastic.

As for the writer seeking for material in the large centres of population, one at least of them has derived not a little good-natured fun from the spectacle of young industrial Scotland, badly cinema struck and seeking to acquire the glittering veneer of Hollywood. Lavinia Derwent was responsible not long ago for the sketch referred to, a masterly vignette on dance halls which includes a glance at a night out at one of the humbler 'pallys' of the west. She observes the Scots lasses, no longer Jeans or Maggies but rejoicing in exotic names culled from the film stars. Preparing for the nights' 'jigging' in the cloakroom they strive determinedly for a glamour foreign to their normal sonsy good looks, taking out the last curler and putting a final dab of 'My Sin' behind the ears. But, says Miss Derwent, 'The conversation . . . takes a slightly couthy turn, as they ask each other: "Here, Veronica, ye micht hae a decko at ma back-seams. An' what's ma hair like?" "Smashin', Marleen. C'mon! there's the band giein' *Jezebel* big licks." '

Nor do their escorts escape her gently malicious pen as they hasten to the dance floor, running a comb through their 'permed' locks. It is all observed with much acuteness, especially in the passage which describes the approach of the young male to the young female:

'Nipping out his cigarette and parking the "dowt" behind his ear, he elbows his way into a strategic position, and with old-world courtesy gives her a dunt on the back, or merely lifts his

eyebrows and jerks his head in the direction of the dance-floor. She needs no second invitation. Away they prance into the *mêlée*, are soon lost in the thick of the scrum.'

The farewell speeches of the lady guests to each other are just as neatly sketched, and delightful in their revelation of the homely Scot peeping through the Hollywood cutie, like a linsey-wolsey petticoat hanging below the hem of a cheap rayon dress. Marlene addresses Dolores:

'"My! ma feet are fair killin' me. Are ye no tired Doloars?" "Ay! no half. Never heed, I'll get a rest at ma work the morn. See ye at the jiggin' at night. Cheerybye, Marleen. Don't do nothing I wouldn't do." '

As for our Scots comedians, few of them now drag in the bawbee or the bottle. They can be funny enough in other ways which Scots audiences will rise to at once. Hear Dave Willis and watch his face when he is told: 'Run! There's a moose loose. It's pawing the ground and snorting with rage.' 'A moose!' he murmurs, his eyes glittering with disbelief, 'pawin' the grund?'

94

How then, shall we portray the comic muse of Scotland? Not as a dowdy grippy woman, living entirely in the kitchen and presenting a coarse red face to the world. Rather perhaps can she be likened to one of Raeburn's old ladies, a wise merry personality who has seen much of humanity, can laugh kindly at its follies, but has little use for conceit or bombast, which she will prick with a few well-chosen words. She can be both aristocratic and democratic, dealing in the wit which brings laughter with the nuts and wine, or retailing with gusto the gleg humour of kitchen and farm-toun. In old age she draws her tartan shawl around her and becomes a little more homely and Scottish in her language and outlook, as do we all if we remain within our own bounds.

'What he could do if he got among the English!' exclaims one of Barrie's characters about an eident lad o pairts. Sometimes we feel the same about our comic muse, who, could they but understand her, would pull them out of the plush, as the old actors say. But perhaps it is better that she stay here. She is less exportable than our whisky and Aberdeen-Angus beef, and even more necessary to our well-being.

An old country minister with an Apocalyptic style of delivery was trying to bring his flock to a full realization of their sins, but saw nothing but apathetic faces as he looked down from the pulpit. One or two of the young folk even seemed to be smiling in a half concealed way.

'Aye ye may lauch noo,' he thundered, 'but when ye're burnin' in the Nethermost Pit ye wull look up and cry oot "Oh Loard, we didna ken, we didna ken!" And the Loard, in His infinite maircy, will look doon on ye an' say, "Weel, ye ken noo!"'

A Galloway laird and his wife had dined with a neighbour who was over hospitable, and in addition to plying them with wine during the meal, had pressed upon them much more than the usual 'one for the road'. It was therefore a tricky business to get home safely, the laird on his horse and his wife perched behind him pillion fashion. By this time my lady was feeling the effects of her potations, and dovered into sleep, until at last she released her grip and slipped off the horse in the darkness. Equally sleepy and well-wined, the laird did not miss her until he got home, when there was a great hue and cry and a search party was sent out. At length its leader found her lying at the ford of the river Urr where it joins to the sea. The incoming tide was actually trickling into her mouth as they reached her, and as she was lifted up from the ground she was heard to murmur politely: 'I canna tak anither drap—neither het nor cauld!'

MY FRIEND ROBERT BURNS

by *Hilton Brown*

THE stock thing to say about Burns is that he was, and is, not
only my friend but everyone's because he had in him something
of and something for each member of mankind. This is perhaps
to exaggerate; he was not so complicated as all that; no man
could be. Neither, however, was he the straightforward
ploughman-poet, lover-drinker, sinner-repenter, Radical-revolu-
tionary that many have made him. It is not going far enough
even to say that he represented, magnified to the scale of
genius, the normal human mixture of surliness and charm,
decency and beastliness, the high mind and the low life, the
fastidious and the coarse, the lure and the repellent. He was a
thoroughly complex character, switching rapidly and caprici-
ously from opposite to opposite; nor was this at all unnatural
because these ups and downs, hots and colds, are typical of the
undiagnosed heart disease from which, during his whole adult
life, he suffered. He was himself intensely interested in these
vagaries and talked about them a great deal.

'My Friend Robert Burns'—no doubt a pretentious title.
How can one call another a friend without knowing him? How
can one know a man who lived nearly two hundred years ago
in an environment and a society scarcely less alien to today's
than the Eskimo or the Polynesian? Pertinent questions. Yet
I feel—and others have felt the same—that I know Burns as I
know no other of the great departed. He is clay and they are
clay but *his* clay can come alive again. I know him and I like
him—at times I love him. I can justify my title therefore to the
extent at least of a one-sided friendship.

If a man says he likes and even loves another, he must give
reasons for it; I have mine—and they are not everybody's. I

know my friend too well to like him in those hours when many have liked him most. For instance, when he is demonstrating his 'independence', which he did too often by making himself a boor to those who, having already decided that he was one, merely shrugged their shoulders as being pleasantly confirmed. I enjoy his company when he is having a glass and a song but not when he is boasting (and lying) about how much he has put away; I know as well as he did the limits imposed upon him by a weak stomach and I know that, in drinking terms of his day, these were soon reached. I admire his eloquence and heat as Jacobin and as Jacobite, but I am all the time aware that he could not really, any more than any other man, be both these at once, and I look on therefore with at best indulgence—a not very friendly feeling from which impatience is never far away. I do not fancy his bawdry because, as bawdry, it is often pretty dull, and others have done the thing much better. I weary of him as the insatiable (and exhibitionist) lover and when, as in his later poems, he becomes also the unrequited, he bores me stiff. Others—many others—have admired him in all these moods; I cannot.

Where he does enslave me is in the example he sets me by his courage. It has been said many times before but let it be said once again—here was a man whose life was one long and losing battle with grinding toil, sickness in its most depressing form, disappointment and balked ambition; yet he is remembered not as a valetudinarian or a whiner but as the prince of good fellows, the very king of companions, one who, instead of drawing upon his friends, poured into them from his own resources hope, encouragement and spirit. In the last black hours at Brow Well he could meet Maria Riddell with 'Madam, have you any commands for the next world?' and when, on his hopeless deathbed in Dumfries, Syme came to see him and took him by the hand, he made, Syme says, a 'wonderful exertion' and exclaimed, 'I am much better today—I shall soon be well again.' Burns faced undismayed the intolerable inquisitions and penances of the Kirk at Mauchline, paying boldly for his bold sin; a brute, of course, might have stood equally unconcerned on the Cutty Stool—but then Burns was no brute but a bundle of nerves. He faced again the New Athenians of Edinburgh calmly and fearlessly; again, a country bumpkin, inflated by his local success, might have done as much—but Burns was neither bumpkin nor inflated; he knew, all too fatally, just where he stood. If courage is the conquest of one's limitations, then Burns's courage was supreme. One bows before it.

And then his kindness—the instant warmth with which he ran to the aid of whatever and whoever he believed to be the persecuted, the downtrodden, the victim of injustice or malice. How he fought and battled for Clarke the schoolmaster of Moffat (whom he scarcely knew) in his war with his Patrons—fought on to eventual victory. His young brother William Burns, 'Hornbook' Wilson, Muir's widow—how many could testify to his ready response to their appeals. Burns's volatile disposition and hair-trigger touchiness did not allow him to keep his friends and sooner or later he quarrelled with most of them; but while they were his friends—Nicol, Sillar, Smith, Richmond—they could have the coat off his back and all the cash in its pockets. He halved his hard-won takings from his Edinburgh Edition by 'lending' his brother Gilbert two hundred pounds to save the family farm at Mossgiel; flush or hard-up—and it was usually the latter—he budgeted five pounds every year for his mother and seven for 'Dear-bought Bess' his first illegitimate daughter. When his uncle Robert died, his two sons and one daughter were taken into the impoverished household at Ellisland without question and for an indefinite period. It is easy to do these things when one is provided with ample funds—though that is not to say that in these circumstances they are always done; when one is battling for every penny against health, weather, a poor farm, an impossible economic system and a hard-hearted society, it is another and a finer story.

Apart from his courage and generosity at levels to which I (and most of us) cannot aspire, I can meet my friend Burns and be delighted with him on lower planes. Is there anyone whose heart is so hard that he cannot rejoice in that very young man of four-and-twenty shutting himself up in the attic at Mossgiel and opening so solemnly and so earnestly his 'Commonplace Book'? 'Observations, Hints, Songs, etc. by Robt. Burness: a man who had little art in making money and still less in keeping it; but was, however, a man of some sense, a great deal of honesty and unbounded goodwill to every creature, rational or irrational.' This same elderly young man has been 'all along a miserable dupe to Love' and has been 'led into a thousand weaknesses and follies by it'. So the book begins, and it ends with the name of Jean Armour—in cypher. All very self-conscious, very disingenuous, very much of a pose? Yes, but is it not for that very reason delightful?

And then the Burns thrown back defeated (though of course never admitting it) on Ellisland, setting up there to be the Nithsdale Horace. He could see himself as Horace of all people —he, Rob Mossgiel! The fluttering little 'philosophies' of one who was the most unphilosophic of men. The wonderful things Horace is to do; the *complete* works' of the British and French dramatists ordered from Edinburgh—and never read; 'a hundred different poetic plans' projected—and ending at that. Horace as his exemplar on one hand, the Miltonic Satan on the other; in which is he more absurdly lovable?

There is so much at which the enemy can sneer but the friend can smile. The Armours are at his heels with their warrants; he must fly to Jamaica—and for a time he persuades himself that fly he really will and perish there he certainly must, and he works himself almost into hysterics. (Sheer dramatization, of course, and nothing more, but how attractive.) . . . The complete rustic (if Edinburgh wanted a Ploughman Poet, by God she should have one!) stamping up and down Smellie's printing-office, in boots and driving-coat, cracking an enormous whip. . . . His fury over the snub administered by the Lass o Balloch-myle—which indeed he deserved not for his forwardness but for the appalling string of clichés with which he had saluted her. . . . Anxious to get on in the Excise and naïvely suggesting to his patron that Mr Leonard Smith might be sacked to provide a vacancy 'as the gentleman, owing to some legacies is quite opulent, and removal could do him no manner of injury'. . . . Writing to his acquaintance to tell them (in the same set and carefully polished formula) how a 'damned Star has all my life usurped my zenith and squinted out the cursed rays of its malignant influences'. . . . Writing so forbearingly to an old busybody in Alnwick who had rebuked and 'advised' him on his immoral and dangerous tendencies. . . . Hiding a stock of quotations in his sleeve and trotting out a 'favourite' at need.

. . . In the last grim days of Dumfries, discovered by Gray the Academy Rector 'explaining to his little boy the English poets from Shakespeare to Collins or storing his mind with examples of heroic virtue'. . . . *Certain* that his founder-ancestor was a Campbell driven out of Argyll because of his Stewart sympathies, *certain* that his ancestors had fought and suffered for the Stewart cause, more than half certain that he would have done the same himself. (And one would say, 'Yes, yes, Robbie', knowing it to be all nonsense.)

He prided himself so on his French; and then one day that mischievous girl Peggy Chalmers (who wouldn't marry him) confronted him with a French lady—and neither could understand one word the other said. (Robbie's 'French'; he rhymed 'amours' with 'Chalmers'; the French lady was not to be blamed.) . . . And his tactlessness was so glorious as to be almost a virtue; bursting out into a 'pointed and decisive' eulogy of Blair's hated rival at Blair's own table; telling Mrs Dunlop, the mother-in-law of two *émigré* aristocrats, that the late King and Queen of France were 'a perjured Blockhead and an unprincipled Prostitute'. What a man!

These are lovable hours at which the friend can smile; there are others, equally poignant, at which he can not. Those 'hypochondriacs' and 'flying gouts' and 'malignant squinancies' on which R.L.S. was so mean-mindedly severe; in the Commonplace Book days Robin is treating these alternately with cold baths and a special prayer to be read when he feels like fainting —all carefully written out in the book. Can *anyone* remain unmoved by that? At Ellisland he is flying to 'the Muses' (sometimes the 'Tuneful Sisters') for refuge from these torments 'which I fear worse than the devil'. In the end he carries them to Brow Well on the Solway—and there they finish him. Among all the contrary moments of his life I never feel nearer to my friend Burns than in those last bitter days at that horrid little resort, condemned by his doctors to wading and bathing in its disgusting mud-and-water, striving thereafter to warm his poor body with the solitary bottle of port the comfortless inn could provide, worrying (quite needlessly) about his bills and his debts, forced on this hopeless course of treatment in which he still must hope. And sitting there game to the last, and calling for ink and paper and posting off to Alec Cunningham and George Thomson a brace of new songs. That was nine days before he died. . . .

'My Friend Robert Burns.' But could I or any of us ever have been Burns's friend? Friendship is give-and-take; he had so much to give, so little to be given. What could one set against that fantastic courage, how could one match the best hours of that inspired brilliance, how could the ordinary cold little human heart array itself against that furnace of glow and warmth? It is possible to admire—marvel—worship—and millions of our kind have done it. But friendship is a level thing between man and man, and who is going to stand himself on a level with Robert Burns?

Not I. Yet I will not withdraw my title because I wish so much with all my heart that it could have been true.

To Dr Hugh Blair

LAWN MARKET, EDINBURGH, 3 *May* 1788.

Reverend and much respected Sir,

I leave Edinburgh tomorrow morning, but could not go without troubling you with half a line, sincerely to thank you for the kindness, patronage, and friendship you have shewn me. I often felt the embarrassment of my singular situation: drawn forth from the veriest shades of life to the glare of remark; and honoured by the notice of those illustrious names of my country whose works, while they are applauded to the end of time, will ever instruct and mend the heart. However the meteor-like novelty of my appearance in the world might attract notice, and honour me with the acquaintance of the permanent lights of genius and literature. . . . I knew very well that my utmost merit was far unequal to the task of preserving that character when once the novelty was over; I have made up my mind that abuse, or almost even neglect, will not surprise me in my quarters. . . .

To Alexander Cunningham   25 *February* 1794.

Canst thou minister to a mind diseased? Canst thou speak peace and rest to a soul tost on a sea of troubles, without one friendly star to guide her course, and dreading that the next surge may overwhelm her? Canst thou give to a frame, tremblingly alive to the tortures of suspense, the stability and hardihood of the rock that braves the blast? If thou canst not do the least of these, why wouldst thou disturb me in my miseries, with thy inquiries after me? . . .

For these two months I have not been able to lift a pen. My constitution and frame were, *ab origine*, blasted with a deep incurable taint of hypochondria, which poisons my existence. Of late a number of domestic vexations, and some pecuniary share in the ruin of these d-mned times—losses which though trifling, were yet what I could ill bear—have so irritated me, that my feelings at times could only be envied by a reprobate spirit listening to the sentence that dooms it to perdition. . . .

Still there are two great pillars that bear us up, amid the wreck of misfortune and misery. The ONE is composed of the different modifications of a certain noble, stubborn something in man, known by the names of courage, fortitude, magnanimity. The OTHER is made up of those feelings and sentiments which however the sceptic may deny them or the enthusiast disfigure them, are yet, I am convinced, original and component parts of the human soul; those *senses of the mind* if I may be allowed the expression, which connect us with, and link us to those awful obscure realities—an all-powerful and equally beneficent God, and a world to come, beyond death and the grave. The first gives the nerve of combat, while a ray of hope beams on the field; the last pours the balm of comfort into the wound which time can never cure.

To Mrs Dunlop

ELLISLAND, 21 *April* 1789.

. . . If you knew my present hurry of building, planning, planting, ploughing, sowing, etc., etc., you would give me great credit for this sheet-ful. Every minute has five minutes' business to do, and every crown has a twenty-shilling errand to run. I have just got a reading of some books I wanted much; and a parcel of Poems, now in the current of subscription, have given me, daily give me, a world of trouble in revising them. They are hopeless trash; but the Authoress is a poor young creature whose forefathers have seen better days; for which consideration I submit to the horrid drudgery. I have over and above the 3rd Vol. of the Scots Songs among my hands, among which will appear some delectable pieces of my Muse's dreams.

To George Thomson

BROW, 4 *July* 1796.

My dear Sir,

I recd your songs: but my health being so precarious nay dangerously situated that as a last effort I am here at a sea-bathing quarters.—Besides my inveterate rheumatism, my appetite is quite gone, & I am so emaciated as to be scarce able to support myself on my own legs.—Alas! is this a time for me to woo the Muses? However, I am still anxiously willing to serve your work; & if possible shall try:—I would not like to see another employed, unless you could lay your hand upon a poet whose productions would be equal to the rest.—You will see my alterations & remarks on the margin of each song.—You may think it hard as to 'Cauld kail in Aberdeen,' but I cannot help it.—My address is still Dumfries.

Farewell! & God bless you!

R. BURNS

REDISCOVERING OUR HERITAGE

by Robert Hurd

LOOKING back over the past twenty-five years, one cannot but notice the gradual change that has come over the attitude of the Scottish public towards the architectural heritage of their own country.

Appreciation of architecture plays little or no part in school *curricula*, and the place allotted to Scottish subjects of any kind, though improving, is still pitifully inadequate. It is scarcely surprising, therefore, that the average Scot can grow up without much experience of looking at buildings anywhere, and little or none of appreciating the architecture of Scotland in particular.

Old buildings have tended therefore to be valued rather for their associations with famous people or with romantic episodes in history: and if they lack either, their chance of survival may, in certain circumstances, prove slender indeed.

Does this matter, one may ask? Is one's architectural background of any moment in daily life? Well, we live in houses, worship in churches, work in offices, factories, studios and farm buildings, and walk about towns and villages every day of our lives: their appearance, therefore, must have an effect on us, consciously or unconsciously. The idiom of our own country is that which comes most naturally to us, as much in architecture as in speech; and unless we can understand and appreciate the best of what has been handed down from past generations we lack the normal means of forming a sound aesthetic judgment, which can in turn be applied to problems of the present day. Apart from that, there is the perennial interest and stimulus to the imagination provided by old buildings as mirrors of a past way of life, and as examples of good craftsmanship.

The work of documentation under official auspices—that is the making of inventories of ancient monuments, was started before the first World War, and has proceeded slowly but steadily, county by county, ever since. The work of conservation of the more notable buildings and ruins by the Ministry of Works has stabilized the condition of many famous places such as Linlithgow Palace and the noble ruins of Melrose, Jedburgh, and Dryburgh. But the care of old buildings of more modest scale, occupied as dwellings, has been fitful and subject both to the constant hazards of wayward and ill-informed public opinion and to the dire effect of the Scottish rating system: and it is here that our losses have been so serious owing to both decay and actual demolition in the interests of public health.

One of the major difficulties—still with us—is to convince members of the public and particularly of local authorities, that what appears to them a tumbledown rickle o stanes is in fact a potentially significant specimen of vernacular architecture either in itself or as part of a group; and that it can be brought back into circulation as dwelling houses, or as some public institution, given the care and thought of a skilled architect and an experienced contractor, sometimes even at less cost than the provision of entirely new buildings with equivalent accommodation.

How often has one battled with local authorities on this issue! One of the earliest controversies in my experience was in 1938 over Tailors' Hall Buildings in the Cowgate of Edinburgh—a magnificent seventeenth century group of Scottish burgh architecture, perfectly capable and well worthy of restoration and conversion into an extension of Heriot-Watt College, but subject to a most determined and unscrupulous campaign for its destruction by the Town Council of the day on the score of road widening which, in fact, has never taken place to this day. The battle for its preservation was carried to the uttermost limits, through the Dean of Guild Court to a Court of Session interdict, with an influentially signed petition organized by the Saltire Society into the bargain, all to no avail, in that particular case.

Contrasting the attitude of Edinburgh Town Council then with their intelligent preservation after the war of the large seventeenth century building at the corner of Lawnmarket and Bank Street, a block devoid of romantic associations or marked

Saved for posterity, Provost Ross's House is one of the few surviving seventeenth century dwellings in Aberdeen

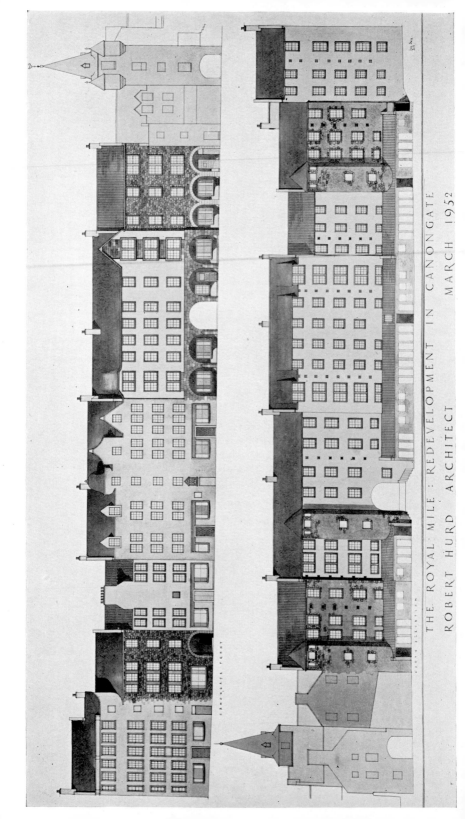

THE ROYAL MILE : REDEVELOPMENT IN CANONGATE

ROBERT HURD ARCHITECT   MARCH 1952

The restored Morocco Land frontage in the Canongate, including (extreme left) a reproduction of the original tenement

features, but nevertheless of prime importance in the street group, one can see at once what an advance there has been, in the capital at least. The bitter pre-war controversy over Tailors' Hall Buildings may well have been an essential preliminary to this change of heart, since confirmed by the treatment, at once conservative and progressive, of the Canongate lower down the Royal Mile, where whole stretches of the street have been rehabilitated by restoration, reconstruction, and new building, for the provision of up-to-date dwelling houses and shops.

Another bitter controversy, in 1953, had to precede the saving and restoration of Provost Ross's house in Aberdeen, one of the very few surviving seventeenth century houses there. Now that the job is finished, of course, every Aberdonian is rightly proud of the result, and fully converted, where previously he was sceptical. Even more difficult, in some ways, was the battle over the simple little groups of old condemned houses forming the street to Dunkeld Cathedral: the most perfect approach, by way of contrast, to the serene gothic of the Cathedral: but by dint of persistence Perthshire County Council were eventually won over so that with their co-operation and that of the Scottish Special Housing Association, the National Trust for Scotland has been able to keep the integrity of this charming traditional group and at the same time provide many good houses urgently required.

The Royal Burgh of Fortrose in the Black Isle, faced with the demolition of a number of mid-eighteenth century condemned houses in its comely streets, decided in 1954, in the face of its Sanitary Inspector's adverse reports, to embark on a programme of rehabilitation, partly to provide the houses they needed, and partly to preserve the character of their streets. Here, there was no controversy, but good will from the start, combined with shrewd common sense from a business point of view.

There are, of course, black spots: the burghers of Banff have perversely declared their intention of demolishing old houses 'merrily' as they please: but we shall see. Public opinion has become much more vocal in the past few years; and even Banff may prove more sensitive to such pressure than one might expect.

A big part has been played in the gradual enlightening of public opinion by the energetic campaign on behalf of 'Little Houses' conducted by the National Trust for Scotland, a body founded in 1931 but at first very wary of being involved in any kind of controversy. The Saltire Society, founded in 1936, with a wider remit on behalf of the whole of the cultural heritage of Scotland, has carried on a continuous programme of public education in the value of good design in both traditional and modern architecture, and the organic relation between the two. The Government, belatedly, introduced in 1950 a good scheme of grants to encourage the rehabilitation of old areas, so that there is no longer any valid reason for a local authority to shirk its responsibilities in this respect: and the Department of Health for Scotland is gradually covering the whole country with its graded lists of old houses which merit retention and restoration. So are we catching up on ignorance and apathy.

One must, however, give credit to the pioneering few who led the way even before the National Trust for Scotland became more militant, or the Saltire Society became active, or the Government took the problem in hand. Of these, apart from a few architects who had the vision to see the value of the old as a springboard for the new, starting with Charles Rennie Mackintosh, Sir Robert Lorimer and Sir Frank Mears, one must honour Sir John Stirling Maxwell of Pollok and the late Marquis of Bute, who by example as patrons of architecture, by speech and by the written word helped to light up a particularly dark place in the mentality of the Scottish people.

108

The New Town has been built upon one uniform plan, which is the only means of making a city beautiful. Great part of this plan as yet remains to be executed, though they proceed as fast as their supplies of money will allow them. The rent of the houses in general amount to £100 per annum, or upwards, and are most of them let to the inhabitants by builders, who buy the ground, and make what advantage they can of it.

The greatest part of the New Town is built after the manner of the English, and the houses are what they call here, 'houses to themselves'. Tho' this mode of living, one would imagine, is much preferable to the former, yet such is the force of prejudice, that there are many people who prefer a little dark confined tenement on a sixth story, to the convenience of a whole house. One old lady fancies she should be lost if she was to get into such a habitation; another that she should be blown away in going over the new bridge; and a third lives in the old style, because she is sure that these new fashions can come to 'nae gude'. But different as these sentiments are in regard to living, they are not more different than the buildings themselves. In no town that I ever saw can such a contrast be found betwixt the modern and ancient architecture, or anything that better merits the observation of a stranger.

   Captain Topham: *Letters from Edinburgh*, 1774

Remember, you must either help your scenery or destroy; whatever you do has an effect of one kind or the other; it is never indifferent. But, above all, remember that it is chiefly by private, not by public, effort that your city must be adorned. It does not matter how many beautiful public buildings you possess, if they are not supported by, and in harmony with, the private houses of the town. Neither the mind nor the eye will accept a new college, or a new hospital or a new institution for a city. It is the Canongate, and the Princes Street, and the High Street that are Edinburgh.

John Ruskin: *Lectures on Architecture and Painting, delivered at the Philosophical Institution, Edinburgh, November 1, 1883*

ALEXANDER SELKIRK, MAN AND MYTH

by N. Melville Shepherd

In the summer of 1821 Sir Walter Scott was the guest of Mr Constable, at Balneil Den, near Kilconquhar, in the Kingdom of Fife, enjoying, among other rural projects, a little gentle carriage exercise to places of antiquarian interest.

On the afternoon in question a natural choice was the village of Largo, for both gentlemen shared an enthusiasm for Defoe's masterpiece, *Robinson Crusoe*, whose hero owed his existence to their fellow-countryman, Alexander Selkirk.

An hour's drive, during which the waters of the Forth were seldom out of sight, brought them on to the cobbles of Largo, the mariner's birthplace.

In a thatched dwelling where Selkirk had stayed, on his return from his island adventure, the visitors were shown his drinking cup and a wooden sea trunk. The owner of the house, a descendant of the family, showed a touching solicitude in preserving the relics. Sir Walter offered to have the coconut-shell cup mounted, circled in silver, and suitably inscribed, a suggestion that was readily adopted.

Today, these two relics are to be seen in our National Museum of Antiquities, and a more evocative exhibit than the old chest that accompanied the marooned mariner to his desert island would be hard to find.

Nothing, apparently, was said to Sir Walter of the existence of Selkirk's birthplace, at the other end of the village. Its discovery was left to another pilgrim, as we shall see.

The visitors then ascended the steep hill, inland, that leads from the sea-town to the kirk-town of Largo. There, in the

110

venerable and picturesque church perched on the foothills of Largo Law, they were deeply interested in a perusal of the Kirk Session's records. These dated from the end of the seventeenth century, and on the closely written parchment pages the parish minister was able to point out several entries in which the Selcraig family figured with a certain lack of restraint.

The decrepit state of the records stirred Sir Walter and Archibald Constable to suggest having them rebound, and it may be thanks to their prompt action that these unique pages have been preserved for posterity. In testimony of this service the volumes bear the inscription 'Rebound at the expence [*sic*] of Archibald Constable of Balneil.'

Both drinking cup and Session records were borne to Edinburgh in due course.

At that time there was in the city a certain John Howell, who, in support of his manifold activities, described himself as a 'Poly-Artist'. This was no vain boast for although book-binding was his trade he was an antiquary and highly skilled in the use of his hands. Howell was a favoured protégé of the Scott family (indeed, when his many Leonardo-like activities failed, it was by their good graces that he became janitor of Edinburgh Academy) so that it is not unreasonable to suppose that it was to the sign of the Poly-Artist that the tattered Kirk records were taken.

Were this so, it would furnish the reason for Howell's decision to inquire into the life of the arresting figure whose identity, with the passage of a century, had been almost eclipsed by the shadow of Defoe's Robinson Crusoe.

He cherished a notion to write a life of Alexander Selkirk, and in so doing rescue the man from the myth he bade fair to become. A word might be said about Howell's notions, for they were as remarkable for their ingenuity as for the field they covered. We have heard of him as a book-binder; to this craft he contributed a method of paper-cutting that was universally adopted. For a time he practised as a doctor 'in an amateur capacity', blending such services—he had an infallible cure for ringworm—with those of a dentist in which rôle he invented the Pompeian dental plate. He restored pictures, mended *objets d'art*, and made meticulous models of the war galleys of the Ancients. In the realm of literature, among other works, he wrote several of Wilson's *Tales of the Borders*. In such a career it was inevitable that a flying machine and a submarine should be attempted. A bat-like plane, launched from the Earthen Mound, now West Princes Street Gardens, grounded almost simultaneously, and cost Howell a broken leg, while a fish-machine in which he rashly submerged himself in the Water of Leith came near to drowning him.

Such a man was John Howell, who set off for Largo by way of the ferry-passage across the Forth and a long jog eastwards along the shore road. He tells us, in the introduction to his excellent little history, that, before undertaking this journey, he had consulted and weighed every available source of information on his subject. The Selkirk story, from the time when the seasoned young buccaneer of twenty-six set sail upon what was to prove a classic adventure, had been more than covered by at least half a dozen chroniclers to most of whom he was a shipmate or at least an acquaintance. Defoe may well have been in the last category, although proof is lacking of the much discussed encounter 'in the house of a Bristol lady'. It is not unlikely that novelist and returned hero met and talked in a seamen's tavern on one side or the other of the Forth, during Defoe's sojourn in Scotland.

The task Howell set himself was to relate the Scottish mariner to the village of his forebears and, in so doing, learn how such a man was bred. It required uncommon courage and endurance to survive four years on a desert island and at the end of that time be given a command in one of the ships that had come to his rescue.

The first visit to Largo did not prove an unqualified success. John Howell was not a privileged person like the Wizard of the North, but he managed to obtain a sight of the relics in the house at the west end of the village where, today, a bronze statue of Selkirk, clad in goat-skins, stands before a reconstruction of what was once the home of his eldest brother, John.

Down at the harbour there were still a few yarns in circulation from which Selkirk emerged as a brash adventurer—a Till Eulenspiegel of the East Neuk. One such is still told of Selkirk's magic bonnet which he had only to turn on his head to travel free by coach and lodge himself gratis at the inns. A Jewish

112

Man and fictional hero blend in the conception of this statue,
erected to Selkirk on the site of his brother's house in Largo

The cup of Alexander Selkirk whilst in Juan Fernandez.
It was mounted on a rosewood foot and stem and provided with
its inscribed silver band through the interest of Sir Walter Scott

fellow-traveller bought the bonnet for ten gold pieces only to find that Selkirk, knowing full well he would travel home penniless, had paid his way in advance.

Disappointed by the lack of serious evidence, Howell returned to Edinburgh and resumed the life of a Poly-Artist. Two years later, however, he had the good fortune to meet, at Canonmills —possibly on the occasion of his submarine test in the Water of Leith—a great-grand-nephew of Alexander Selkirk's.

This old dominie, possessed of a lively intelligence, and an excellent memory, was found to have treasured every available bit of family lore. With this enthusiastic guide Howell once more crossed to Largo and explored in his company every corner that could furnish the sought-after material. Old John Selkirk was the proud possessor of his great-grand-uncle's flip can ('flip' was the sailorman's heartening mixture of beer and spirits) which had served him—in a teetotal capacity—on his island. It bore an inscription—

Alexander Selkirk, this is my one
When you me take on board of ship
Pray fill me full of Punch or Flip

Walking over the straggling cobbles of Temple, Largo and Drummochy which constitute the sea-girt part of the parish, Howell visited once more the house of the relics. This time he was shown an upper room, where, after his return in 1714, the mariner had lived solitary, preferring the company of two cats to that of his relatives. West of the old stone harbour the visitors ascended the steeply mounting ground of that part of the village known as Drummochy, where Lower Largo fades into limitless sand-dunes. A point of interest was the Craggy Wall (now incorporated in the railway embankment) in the lee of which still stand the most westerly cottages in the hamlet. The eastmost of these two semi-detached dwellings was the home of John Selcraig and his wife, Euphan Mackie. Here it was that their seventh son, Alexander, saw the light and heard the first sound of the sea.

The sturdy, thick-walled cottage is harled and whitewashed; the roof is of faded red pantiles but may well have been thatched in former days.

It is typical of its period, though records are no longer in

113

existence to fix that as the late seventeenth century. The double cottage has, for more than a century, served as coach-house, stable, and latterly garage to the pleasant old house in whose grounds it stands. For twenty years the present writer looked out on the Firth of Forth from the windows of this dwelling whose first recorded owner is Ebenezer Coutts, factor to the Lundin of that ilk.

During the late war, when an air-raid shelter was in the course of construction, there came to light, between house and cottages, what appeared to have been piggeries in front of the Selcraig dwelling. In one of the two wills left by Alexander, he mentions the 'outhouses, garden-yards, and orchard', all of which could have been accommodated on the sunny, seaward slope leading down to the salt-pans. Here on this grassy incline was John Selcraig's tan-yard, for he combined the trades of cobbler and tanner, to which several of his sons were thirled.

Above the cottage, high up amid the rough scrub of the Craggy Wall, Howell was shown the spot long identified as the 'look-out' of the returned mariner, the site of a hut reminiscent of his days on Juan Fernandez. From this Fife eyrie he viewed the sweep of the Forth and lived again, in retrospect, his long, empty, Pacific hours.

Filled with such imaginings and every available fact, Howell returned to Edinburgh and set about compiling his little history of Alexander Selkirk, the only one in which subsequent writers have been able to quarry. Very little factual matter has been added with the years—*The Real Robinson Crusoe*, by R. L. Mégroz, yielding further information only in respect of the lamentable postscript to the mariner's life.

By the publication of his book, in 1829, Howell only partly succeeded in rescuing man from myth. His natal village has contributed to this confusion by the presence, on the harbour, of a hostelry dedicated to Robinson Crusoe himself. On its picturesque sign is the undoubted portrait of the rival rover, the land-lubber from York, child of an English brain, who borrowed our hero's adventures, and beat his record of residence on a desert island by some twenty-three years.

To be fair, it must be admitted that, without Defoe's genius in incorporating Selkirk's island life in his unrivalled adventure classic, the memory of the Largo mariner might not have survived furth his native village. And even there, for all Howell's brave defence of a wayward, hot-tempered loon, there is sadly little on record that redounds to Selkirk's credit.

His first recorded appearance, at the age of thirteen, is in an armed mob led through the kirkyard by his eldest brother, in an attempt to debar the minister from entering his church, a manœuvre that succeeded so well that the parish priest fled the district. His pulpit was refilled, in the course of time, but evidently not to Alexander's satisfaction, for his second mention in the Session's records is on a charge of 'undecent beaiver' which took the form of 'thrawing a mouth' at the minister. For this offence he was commanded to appear before the congregation and be publicly admonished. Under the date due for him to 'compeer' before his judges, the faded ink records that the mouth-thrawer is 'away to ye seas'.

There is surely something disproportionate in the fact that, rather than face the Kirk Session, Selkirk spent the next five years with the buccaneers of the Spanish Main—an exploit of which little is known.

Back home again, at the cottage in Drummochy—a bronzed man of ox-like strength, twenty-four years of age—Selkirk tried for a year or two to settle down to the life his father would have chosen for him. His mother, we are told, had always cherished dreams for her seventh son, so that in choosing the sea by way of a road to adventure, he had Euphan Mackie on his side. Perhaps it was from her that he first heard stories of Largo's early hero, Admiral Sir John Wood, whose ships had beaten the English Admiral Bull after two long days' struggle. Scots and English galleons, out there on the Forth, had been locked in deadly combat, while the sound of their ordnance could be heard by the Largo folk whose kin manned the 'Yellow Frigate'. Memories of such childhood tales may have been siren voices in the ears of the reluctant cobbler, but the event that caused his next flight was more prosaic.

The domestic interlude at Drummochy had a sad end, due no doubt to the notorious family temper and a rather too communal existence, even for the eighteenth century. Cooped up together, the splenetic Selcraigs one day rent the air of Drummochy with their cries. Andrew (who appears to have been

what is referred to as 'no wyce') served his thirsty brother
Alexander with a draught of salt water—the ballad-like story
is told in vivid detail in the Session's records. In a great rage,
the one-time buccaneer felled his brother. Here their father
intervened, and by sitting on Alexander, whom he had succeeded in tripping up, prevented him from reaching down his
Spanish pistol from the wall and shooting up the home.

Soon the whole family were involved, except the mother,
who wisely fled rather than see her beloved seventh son get the
worst of it. The result of this unseemly brawl was the Stool of
Repentance and public disgrace for Alexander.

This time, the season being unpropitious, he was forced to
wait until the following spring before he could join Captain
Dampier's expedition to the South Seas. Dampier's twin ships
called themselves privateers but the only difference Selkirk
could have found between his new and former shipmates was
that between a thief armed with a letter of introduction and one
without.

That Selkirk (the family name for the first time is so spelled)
was an experienced seaman is made manifest by the fact that
he was Sailing Master, or mate, in the *Cinque Ports* under
Captain Pickering whose untimely death promoted to his place
a man who was Selkirk's sworn enemy. Captain and mate
quarrelled so notably, in a ship where strife habitually prevailed,
that in the end Selkirk—protesting, with a last flash, that he
preferred it—was marooned on the island of Juan Fernandez,
in the South Pacific.

There, his four years and two months have been more than
adequately chronicled. Once Selkirk became 'news' his adventures were related by several contemporaries. Howell incor-
porates them all. The marooned man's first terrible loneliness
and despair; his new-found comfort in the spiritual faith of his
childhood; the growing sense of health and vigour such as he
had never before known; his warm attachment to the animals
that shared his daily life—out of which endless images comes one
that must always haunt the imagination. Was there ever a
stranger sight beneath the Southern Cross than that of goats
and cats dancing to the strains of a Scottish psalm from the
rusty throat of their ring-master, he in goat-skins and 'looking
wilder than their first owners'?

116

But the idyll was not to outlast Selkirk's rescue. The prison shades were to fall on the Child of Nature.

One spring morning in 1704, a richly dressed stranger arrived in Largo. It was the Sabbath, and the cottage he sought was empty, the faithful having gone to kirk in the upper village. There, by way of Lundie Mill, the stranger took his way, and tip-toed quietly to a seat, near that of the Selcraig family. His mother was the first to recognize in the prosperous stranger her seventh son. Sermon or no sermon she followed him to the kirkyard, the family behind her, and the faithful bringing up the rear, so that 'Finally, my brethren' fell upon a skailed kirk.

In spite of the natural joy of reunion Selkirk soon found that to settle down was an impossibility. Proximities irked him; he sought some degree of privacy under his brother John's roof. The lonely beach beyond Temple became his haunt, as it was that of the rabbits and the wild-fowl. But he was restless, and soon, without warning, he stole away, taking no material belongings, and leaving his parents in life-possession of the cottage at the Craggy Wall which he had purchased with some of the fruits of his privateering.

With him he took pretty Sophia Bruce, a local lass, whom he persuaded to leave the care of her mother's cow, and to set off for London with her promised husband.

It would be agreeable to end on this poetic note, but the rest of the narrative is prose. Arrived in London, Selkirk drew up a will, leaving as his sole legatee, his 'loveing friend, Sophia Bruce, of the Pel-mel'. With her, on his subsequent returns from sea, he appears to have resided at that vague address without, however, consolidating her position—a grievous over-sight for Sophia, as events proved.

A final voyage in 1721, as Lieutenant in His Majesty's Ship *Weymouth*, brings us to the bald entry in her log book 'Alexander Selkirk. Deceased.'

Sophia Bruce's claim to the dead man's pay was quashed, dramatically, by one Frances Candis, or Hall, Innkeeper of Oreston, in the parish of Plymstock, Devon, who produced legal proof of her own marriage in 1720 to Lieutenant Selkirk of the *Weymouth*. A will in her favour was proved, and poor Sophia sinks without trace from the story except for an appeal to a London clergyman for Parish Relief 'being reduced to want by reason of this hard season', and signed, with touching persistance, 'Sophia Selchrig'.

Fortunately the discovery of this seamy postscript is of recent date—being the find of Mr Mégroz—so that John Howell was saved further embarrassment in his gallant attempt to extricate man from myth.

The island abounds in goats, which he shot while his powder lasted, and afterwards caught by speed of foot. At first he could only overtake kids; but latterly, so much did his frugal life, joined to air and exercise, improve his strength and habits of body, that he could run down the strongest goat on the island in a few minutes, and tossing it over his shoulders, carry it with ease to his hut. . . .

With these capabilities, hunting soon became his chief amusement. It was his custom, after running down the animals, to slit their ears, and then allow them to escape. The young he carried to the green lawn beside his hut, and employed his leisure hours in taming them. They in time supplied him with milk, and even with amusement, as he taught them as well as his cats to dance; and he afterwards declared that he never danced with a lighter heart or greater spirit anywhere to the best of music than he did to the sound of his own voice with his dumb companions.

During his stay he built himself two huts with the wood of the pimento-tree, and thatched them with a species of grass that grows to the height of seven or eight feet upon the plains and smaller hills, and produces straw resembling that of oats. The one was much larger than the other, and situated near a spacious wood. This he made his sleeping-room, spreading the bed-clothes he had brought on shore with him upon a frame of his own construction; and as these wore out, or were used for other purposes, he supplied their place with goats' skins. His pimento bed-room he used also as his chapel; for here he kept up that simple but beautiful form of family worship which he had been accustomed to in his father's house. Soon after he left his bed, and before he commenced the duties of the day, he sung a psalm or part of one, then he read a portion of Scripture, and finished with devout prayer. In the evening, before he retired to rest, the same duties were performed. His devotions he repeated aloud to retain the use of speech, and for the satisfaction man feels in hearing the human voice, even when it is only his own. The greater part of his days was spent in devotion; for he afterwards said, with tears in his eyes, that 'He was a better Christian while in his solitude than ever he was before, and feared he would ever be again.'

As to his clothing it was very rude. Shoes he had none, as they were soon worn out. This gave him very little concern, and he never troubled himself in contriving any substance to supply their place. As his other clothes decayed he dried the skins of the goats he had killed to convert into garments, sewing them with slender thongs of leather which he cut for the purpose, and using a sharp nail for a needle. In this way he made for himself a cap, jacket, and short breeches. The hair being retained upon the skin gave him a very uncouth appearance; but in this dress he ran through the underwood, and received as little injury as the animal he pursued. Having linen cloth with him, he made it into shirts, sewing them by means of his nail and the threads of his worsted stockings, which he untwisted for that purpose. Thus rudely equipped, he thought his wants sufficiently supplied, fashion having no longer any empire over him.

Howell: *The Life and Adventures of Alexander Selkirk*

The word 'tartan' is derived from the French 'tiretaine' and in its original form it meant a particular type of cloth quite irrespective of any colour. This original meaning of the word was in use up to recent times and in the Dress Regulations of the British Army plain dark cloth used for trousers is called 'tartan'. The green cloth worn by the Rifle Regiment was also referred to as 'tartan'.

J. Telfer Dunbar, from *Ciba Review* (Basle, June 1951)

The Plad, wore only by the Men, is made of fine Wool, the Thread as fine as can be made of that kind; it consists of divers Colours, and there is a great deal of ingenuity requir'd in sorting the Colours, so as to be agreeable to the nicest Fancy. For this reason the Women are at great pains, first to give an exact pattern of the Plade, upon a piece of Wood, having the number of every thread of the stripe on it. The length of it is commonly seven double Ells; the one hangs by the middle over the left Arm, the other going round the Body, hangs by the end over the left Arm also. The right hand above it is to be at liberty to do anything upon occasion. Every Isle differs from each other in their fancy of making Plaids, as to the Stripes in Breadth and Colours. This Humour is as different thro' the main Land of the Highlands in so far that they who have seen those Places is able, at the first view of a Man's Plaid, to guess the place of his Residence.

Martin: *Description of the Western Isles of Scotland*, 1703

120

HUNTING THE TARTAN

by J. Telfer Dunbar

I THINK that I was probably irritated into being a student of early costume and a collector of ancient Highland dress and tartans. As I became aware of the modern vestiges of Scottish costume around me I also became more and more confused by an evident hotch-potch of true traditional pride and bogus sentiment. The sight of a kilted regiment gave me as much pleasure as 'Highland' dancers with flying curls, foams of lace and dangling medals gave me pain. Surely the national dress of the Scottish highlander must have some authentic roots? Were they being strangled by commercialism and 'le tourisme' just as I had been near to strangulation when made to wear an Eton collar with my Sunday kilt? Whatever and wherever these roots were I determined to find out.

Fortunately my Eton collar was eventually discarded and more fortunately my kilt was not—I have always been of the opinion that nothing becomes a man less than a new kilt. Admittedly mine had by now become too short and I am reminded of the observation made in 1822 by the noble duchess regarding the shortness of King George the Fourth's kilt which brought the rejoinder from her companion: 'Never mind, His Majesty's visit is short too, so the more we see of him the better.'

The years passed and my schoolboy kilt had at last to be discarded. I immediately took its successor on a climbing holiday in Skye and by the time I got home it had a fine air of antiquity. I shall never forget that holiday and the memory of that most lovely island will always remain. It was there that I saw my first real tartan and realized how utterly unlike it was to any of the so-called tartans I had seen before. However, I was to experience another first occasion before I reached the island. Shortly after I boarded the steamer at Kyle of Lochalsh I became involved in my first game of chance. We stood in a circle in the hold whilst above our heads an unhappy cow was lowered aboard from a derrick. Slowly she rotated against the June sky and then as her feet touched the deck a shout of delight went up from the waiting circle around her. Her blunt end was directly opposite my right-hand neighbour. 'All right,' he cried, 'there's no argument—the drinks are on me.' The game required no explanation. Probably it was my request for lemonade that aroused my host's interest but the conversation got on to tartans and when we parted company I had the address of an old lady at Sligachan who would show me a piece of 'the real stuff'.

That night I slept at Portree in what had been a refuge for the Prince in 1746 and was now a large hotel advertising on its brochure 'Basin of Soup, 1/-' and 'Acetylene Gas Installation'. The following evening I had arrived at Sligachan and was seated before a peat fire watching my hostess unwrapping with gentle hands a web of tartan that seemed to fill the room with sad beauty as the light of the flames caught its lovely colours. This great belted plaid which had been clothing by day and bedding by night was of a large and complicated pattern, hard of texture and soft of colour. This was no 'clan' tartan of 'authentic colours'. These were the colours of the hills and the glens. An exhausted refugee might lie on the open slopes and, in its warm protection, be invisible to the hunting Redcoats. As I left I thanked my hostess not only for the privilege of handling such a treasure but also for making me resolve to search my country and endeavour to collect and preserve these elusive relics of part of our national heritage.

My search has taken me far and wide—from the private bedrooms of the Sobieski Stuarts to the junk shops and barrows of the Gallowgate. My reception has been varied and I have had to play many parts and in consequence experience many aspects of human nature. I have been regarded as a rag-and-bone man and on one occasion I overheard myself being exalted to the dignity of 'a professor from wan of the Universeries'. Not many years ago I remember being told by a friend in Inverness about a fine pair of early eighteenth century trews which were for sale in a local antique shop. 'Don't wear your kilt,' he advised.

Seldom have men donned a garb so effective as the Highland
dress in its heyday, worn here by the Hon. William Gordon of
Fyvie (1745-1816)

Two red tartans of similar type and colour are shown in this interesting portrait of a young girl dating from about 1745.

'They will think you are an English tourist and put up the price.'

One of the greatest joys of collecting was the association it brought with people and places. Of the former my greatest debt is to the late Major Mackay Scobie. Not only did he bring together the wonderful collection housed in our Scottish United Services Museum, but also during his long curatorship he gave generously of his knowledge to all young students. Our understanding of a major part of Scotland's history is due to his untiring efforts. A true Highlander with knowledge of the language, music and customs of the Gael, he had an abiding love for his native land. There can be few national museums which, after eighteen years, had built up an international reputation without even the assistance of a telephone or a typewriter. To stand beside him on the Half-Moon Battery above a sleeping Edinburgh after his twenty-four hour day was done was an experience to be remembered.

In the Highlands and the Islands I became increasingly aware of the generosity of the Highland heart. The courtesy of the croft was such a contrast to the artificial 'manners' of the larger hotel. Poverty was seldom an excuse for lack of hospitality. Often I was an unknown stranger who would never be met again but often the farther I was away from 'civilization' the closer would my chair be to the fire. Will this natural generosity survive the widening circle of the tourist trade?

To obtain a full understanding of my subject it was essential that I should learn the rudiments of spinning, weaving and dyeing in the eighteenth century manner. This I enjoyed with the exception of the last of these arts. In the fourteenth century manuscript *Decretals of Gregory*, a woman is depicted in an illumination receiving cloth from the dyer. She takes it in one hand whilst holding her nose with the other and my sympathies are entirely with her. Few recipes of the old Highland organic dyes have survived and it has been regarded as rather romantic to refer to them as 'secret'. My own conclusion is that many of them were 'lost' owing to reticence, on the part of the old people who had used them, to repeat some of their ingredients to 'genteel' folklorists and collectors. Even St. Ciaran's mother ordered him to retire when she was preparing woad and if the legend is correct her dye turned cats and dogs blue!

The folk-lore associated with the making of early textiles in the Highlands forms a fascinating subject awaiting specialized study. The genuine old poems, stories and songs will not survive much longer. Even what we can save of them now is mostly but a dead shadow. I remember having played some of my tape recordings at a lecture in Edinburgh and being complimented on preserving the old spinning and waulking songs. The compliment was lost as I suddenly became aware of the rightness of the expression 'preserve'. I seemed to see rows of bottles of fruit surrounded by syrup and seen through glass. Could one even begin to compare this with the living apples and plums and berries swinging and dancing in the sunlight?

My researches have not always been with the living. A great deal of evidence regarding the early costume and armour of our ancestors is preserved on the lovely sculptured stones of western Scotland. I remember one sunny afternoon when I sat eating my lunch with my back against the effigy of an ancient warrior chief. A small sandy man approached and entered into conversation. He glanced at the large sheet of paper lying on the grass and I explained the method whereby I had made a rubbing off the stone effigy. As he was rather silent I went on to explain— as simply as I could—the intricacies of stone working and the skill required by the artist in stone. After a while I felt that the conversation had become rather one-sided and by way of giving him an opening I asked him if he lived in the district. 'Oh yes,' he replied, 'I'm the local stonemason.'

It was in like manner that I made a friendship in Oxford. I had taken my wife to visit the Bodleian Library and was describing to her the construction of some very fine sixteenth century bindings. A gentleman at her side seemed interested and in order that he should not remain ignorant I included him in my conversation. Feeling rather proud of the way in which I had reduced a rather complicated technique into simple terms I suggested to him that such matters were of great interest. He agreed and added: 'Allow me to introduce myself; I am Librarian here.' As he later showed us some of the library's great treasures I remained unusually silent.

It was of course inevitable that I should receive many interesting and amusing letters in the course of my research work. Many inquiries came from distant quarters of the world and I gradually began to envisage a number of fervent Scots in far-away places fiercely defending the antiquity and superiority of their national dress against all comers. It was argued by one that to make a pair of trousers out of fig leaves was an impossibility and that in consequence we must attribute the invention of the kilt to none other but Adam. By another interesting hypothesis it was maintained that Joseph's coat of many colours was the earliest reference to tartan. I received several soulful appeals from correspondents seeking the 'right' to wear a clan tartan and I often wonder if a spinster lady living in the far north realized that the fact of her being domiciled in the Highlands was being quoted as the 'right' for a distant relative in the United States to decorate her 'parlor' in Buchanan tartan. There is, of course, the classical case of the coloured gentleman in the kilt whose claim to Scottish blood was the fact that his great-great-grandfather had eaten a missionary from Nairn.

In a more serious vein I remember with pride many Scots who spent long years with me as prisoners-of-war in Japanese jungle camps. At a time when our worldly possessions consisted of a few rags and a battered mess-tin they preserved as their greatest treasure a faded Highland bonnet or a tattered kilt. These were not for wear. They were kept with faith and hope for the great day when we would be free men again. Surely such relics deserve to be preserved in our memories as symbols of pride in our native land at its truest and best.

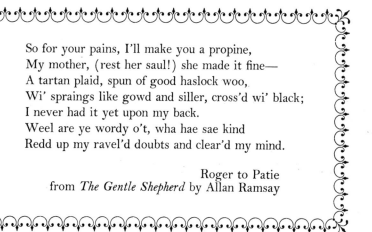

So for your pains, I'll make you a propine,
My mother, (rest her saul!) she made it fine—
A tartan plaid, spun of good haslock woo,
Wi' spraings like gowd and siller, cross'd wi' black;
I never had it yet upon my back.
Weel are ye wordy o't, wha hae sae kind
Redd up my ravel'd doubts and clear'd my mind.

Roger to Patie
from *The Gentle Shepherd* by Allan Ramsay

125

KINTYRE

Leaving those men, whose hearts
are hearths that have no fire,
my greetings westward go
to lovely long Kintyre.

Her uplands draw my thoughts,
till over lands and seas
my dreamings go like birds
that seek the leafy trees.

Of names sweet to the mouth,
of names like the sounding sea,
for my delight alone
I'll write this litany.

Roaig and Airigh Fhuar,
words from some fairy tale,
the Grianan and Davaar,
Carradale, Sunadale.

These on my mouth, I walk
among grey walls and chill,
these are a flame to warm,
a sain against all ill.

from *Wind on Loch Fyne* by George Campbell Hay

THE GARDEN OPENING

by Naomi Mitchison

O n the coldest evening in February I hear the telephone and stumble into the icy telephone room, so as to be asked to give a date in July for my garden opening. After last year I had fully intended not to have it again this year. Just as I also intended the year before. 'All right,' I say gloomily, 'the last Wednesday in July, and let's hope it isn't the same date as the Women's Guild sale in Campbeltown *this* time.' Shall I have a stall with flowers and vegetables? I can't really imagine that there will ever be any flowers again out of the frost-locked ground, but I agree, and to have a dance in the house that evening. And forty per cent for the village hall? Yes, certainly, I say. We have at last built the extension to our village hall which we weren't able to build during the war, and of course we are in debt again. The main thing, however, is that some of the village hall management committee will come and help. I couldn't do without them!

July. Oh well, lots of time till July, I think, hurrying back to my log fire. But only too soon July will come.

Scotland's gardens are opened throughout the summer for the District Nurses' pension fund, the National Trust, and any local charity or good object that the owner may like to name. Shoals of people come along. The owner is all dressed up, madly trying to be polite to everyone. Only those who have done it themselves know the work and worry that's gone into it. One has teas, of course, and one must arrange to have them indoors if it is wet. Numbers are as unpredictable as weather. It may be fifty teas, or a hundred and fifty, but usually there are depressing slabs and sponges left over and piles of sandwiches curling at the edges which one tries to palm off on one's helpers.

The flowers should be picked the evening before, once the sun is off them. One dives into the damp, midgy backs of borders and brings in armfuls which those who don't like midges can then make up into shilling bunches and put into jam jars. People like flowers they know, and will avoid the branch of some interesting rare shrub in favour of a bunch of sweet peas as like as possible to what might be found in a shop. The soft fruit must be picked, wet or fine, the same morning. Fruit and cream is always popular. I borrow cups and saucers from the village hall, as well as one of those monumental urns which take hours to heat. Our village hall is an important part of Carradale life. We had a lovely plan, but it had to be cut owing to war-time restrictions. That meant there was no way from the stage to any kind of green room; play acting lagged. But now we have two handy committee rooms, a door, and an amateur dramatics group. The district nurse holds a mother's clinic in one room, distributes orange juice and weighs babies. In the other the County Library books will be housed as soon as the new shelves are up. There isn't a family in the village which doesn't borrow books, and we don't need to worry about comics when the school children can and do borrow books, sometimes as many as three a week. They start with the sillier school and adventure stories, but soon get on to natural history, crafts, Kon-Tiki and Everest. It is not so long since Argyll had no County Library, and there were those who considered it unnecessary extravagance: the Bible and the daily newspapers were surely enough for anyone? But, with an enthusiastic County Librarian at Dunoon and plenty of interested, unpaid help, it has forged ahead.

Some of the hall committee's daughters and nieces come and help to gather raspberries and currants, and top and tail the little yellow gooseberries, sweet as honey, not to be bought in shops and growing on the prickliest of bushes. There will be some organizing of penny traps—treasure hunts, crowning the shilling and so on. But most important of all, someone firm must be at each entrance before the visitors begin to come, as they are sure to come, a good hour before the appointed time. One year an enterprising small boy collected for himself quite a few shillings before the official gate minders turned up. The earliest comers all bring hungry

children and empty baskets in case there is a bargain to be snapped up.

For of course there are a few bargains, especially among the raffles. Did I say raffles? No, no indeed, the polisman will be after hearing us! They are tests of skill, but nothing so easy as the weight of a cake, since there are housewives who can do that to an ounce, but how many strawberries in a basket (which has been partly stuffed with moss), how many currants in a currant loaf, and the like. Come on, come on, you may win that very exciting embroidered tea cosy which was last seen being a prize at the Life Boat dance in Tobermory. You may win that box of rather nasty chocolates. Or of course you may win a salmon. Because, the night before, I shall have been out with a net.

It was the poachers who taught me how to use a net, and some of the magic is out of it now we are all so old and respectable. But still one must move cautiously and quietly, for salmon, like keepers, are quick to hear a footstep crunching on gravel or a raised voice. Sometimes we use the net as a drag and sometimes as a plash net; the methods are rather different, and one must use one's judgment according to the state of the tide and the direction of the wind.

In June and July the salmon come into the bay, crowding up round the mouth of the river, waiting for a spate when they can get up into the pools. If one rows across here on a still night they turn and flash below one, glowing with phosphorescence and looking even bigger than they are. But a still night is bad for netting; one needs a ripple at least on the surface to cover what one is doing. Usually one person waits on the beach with the end of the net, while the others row out, shooting the net over the stern of the boat, trying to make as little noise as possible on the gunwale with the corks. The one on the beach walks on a little in the direction of the boat, his feet—or her's!—momentarily marked out by the same phosphorescent glitter that lies on the fish. The boat makes a wide circle out and then comes back to land. If the net is used as a drag, they jump out with the end of their rope and both sides of the net are pulled in quickly and evenly, trying to keep the sole of the net, with the weights on it, close to the ground, so that the salmon will not be able to dart underneath and escape. The net has to be well in before you can tell whether there is anything in the bag. But then there are startling pulls and jerks and in a minute you will see a heave up and the surface broken by a netted fish trying to get away. Pull out the bag of the net with a rush and well up the shore, keeping the struggling silver rolled in it!

There may be one or two good-sized fish, as well as grilse and sea-trout, but the smallest will have got away, since we use the wide—and legal!—salmon mesh. Often there are little flatties, dabs and soles and bright-spotted plaice. If they are really small, throw them back. They will recover and you can watch them wavering and rippling their way back into safe waters. The big salmon leap and struggle in one's hands, and often enough, if one leaves them a moment on the beach, they will get away into the sea again. But we need a good basketful for the sale.

If the net is to be used as a plash, the object is to scare the salmon into it so that they will be meshed. Once a big loop of net has been made between boat and shore, the ones in the boat beat on the surface of the water with the oars and those on shore throw stones, trying to drive the fish into charging the net. Then the boat rows back along the inner side of the curve of the net, hauling in, disentangling the fish and throwing them back into the boat. This way you get mostly big fish, and no flatties.

Of course, you may strike a blank. The fish have moved. They may have heard you, or there may be something about the temperature or feeding conditions which has taken them elsewhere. We have two or three bits of the beach which seem best. It does not spoil the river at all when done with discretion. Nor, of course, does discreet poaching, as every keeper knows. The difficulty is that poachers aren't always discreet. Those who want a fish for their tea are one thing, and they get it, all over Scotland, and everyone the best of friends. But when you have the thing on a big scale, with money coming into it, then it's different—as every decent poacher knows!

But here are the salmon, which we are about to raffle—no, to offer as prizes for competitions of skill. Any that are over will be auctioned. No, the second prize is a set of hand-painted doilies. . . .

In the evenings we dance. With luck I shall be able to get hold of an accordionist, in fact I have a plan for inveigling an accordionist on to the village hall committee. We also try and sell off whatever cakes and lemonade have been left over. And sometimes of course we raffle a salmon. It is getting late for anyone to notice.

Throughout the day we have had a variety of helpers, young and old. They will all manage to be there for the time when we count our takings and try to remember what the flower stall made last year and whether it was Mrs Campbell's or Mrs Macintosh's cake which did so extra well. The summer visitors are taken with decorations, but we, the locals, know who our best bakers are. The children who have been in charge of the side-shows bring in a staggering weight of pennies. And as often as not there will be a donation from someone. For the garden opening is a social event. Everyone would miss it if, one year, I lived up to my determination not to have it again. And I suppose I might even miss it myself.

An antiquary in a walled city in Burgundy once presented me with a tattered piece of music. It was one of a series of French historical marches and was said to have been written for the occasion of Joan of Arc's Triumphal Entry to the Cathedral of Rheims for the sacring of the Dauphin.

I carried the leaf of music back to Scotland before playing it. Here it was that I discovered that in spite of its fifteenth century dress it was none other than the Auld Tune—the tune our soldiers sang at Bannockburn: sixteenth century lovers knew it as the aubade 'Hey, noo the day daws, the joly cock craws'; a later era made it a drummer's song called 'Hey tutti taitie' but it was Robert Burns who elevated it to be a national clarion in 'Scots wha hae wi' Wallace bled'.

Who can trace its pedigree? It may already have been a veteran at Bannockburn, and what more natural than that the Maid's Scots archers swung to its lilt on the roads of France? If, as is believed, a Scottish hand painted Joan's banner what more likely than that a fellow-in-arms lent our Auld Tune to the royal trumpeters for that high moment in French history?

N. Melville Shepherd

Your common minstrels has no tune
Bot 'Now the day daws', and 'In to June';
Cunninger men maun serve Saint Cloun,
And ne'er to other craftis claim:
    Think ye not shame
To hauld sic mowers on the moon,
    In hurt and slander of your name?

William Dunbar (? 1460-1520)
from *To the Merchants of Edinburgh*

HEY TUTTI TAITIE

by Tom M. McCourt

A TRUMPET tune that may have been sounded by Robert Bruce's army at the battle of Bannockburn! Such was the tradition associated with this tune, and we have Burns's own word for it that it was a widespread, firmly held one in eighteenth century Scotland.

There is, however, absolutely no evidence in support of this theory nor, from the very nature of the case, can we expect any. Of the instruments of that time we know something of their shape and possibilities from general writings, carvings and other illustrations, but of the music played on them we have nothing, since this was not written down but handed on from player to player by oral tradition.

Whether we accept the story as a possibility or regard it as a pleasing fiction matters little so far as this tune is concerned. One thing at least is fairly certain. I think it can be more or less taken for granted that this tune to which we now sing 'Scots wha hae' and 'The land o the leal' was originally a trumpet tune. It bears all the marks of one, it has the distinctive dotted rhythm associated with such music and, in its simplest form known to us, the first line consists of a single repeated note rising at the end to the keynote a fourth above, another typical trumpet feature found even in present-day calls such as 'Reveillé'.

The title itself imitates the sound of a trumpet,

> When you hear the trumpets sound
> *Tutti taitie* to the drum,

and the word *Hey* at the beginning in conjunction with the rhythm of the melody suggests that the words were pronounced with the first syllables short and the accent on the second, *tutti taitie*, which makes it an even closer imitation of the sound of that instrument. In some dictionaries *tutti* is compared with *toot*, as in Barbour's phrase, *the tutilling of a horne*, but it seems much more likely that it was always pronounced with the short vowel as in *ugh*, in which case these might have been the actual syllables used in sounding the tune on the instrument. The fact that this was probably the melody to which the song, 'The day daws', was formerly sung suggests that it might have been used as a 'Reveillé'.

Whether or not the air is a descendant, several times removed, of that used at Bannockburn is of little importance from a musical point of view. Handed down from generation to generation, as it must have been, by oral tradition, the tune would have been so changed with the passing fashions and styles of the various periods, as well as by the personal taste and fancy of the players themselves, that it would soon have become quite different and completely unrecognizable. Even in the printed books of the later eighteenth and earlier nineteenth centuries it is found in a variety of forms, according to the words to which it is set or the instrument for which it is adapted.

The one thing that really matters is that it was this supposed connection with Bannockburn that fired Burns's enthusiasm and

134

inspired him to produce the song, 'Scots wha hae', that song of which Carlyle writes, 'So long as there is warm blood in the heart of Scotchman or man, it will move in fierce thrills under this war-ode; the best, we believe, that was ever written by any pen.'

Burns's own account of the origin of the song is found in a letter written in 1793 to the Edinburgh lawyer, George Thomson, in which he sends the poem for inclusion in Thomson's book of Scottish songs. Here he writes, '. . . I am delighted with many little melodies, which the learned Musician despises as silly and insipid.—I do not know whether the old air, 'Hey tutti taitie', may rank among this number; but well I know that, with Fraser's Hautboy, it has often filled my eyes with tears.—There is a tradition which I have met with in many places in Scotland, that it was Robert Bruce's March at the battle of Bannock-burn.—This thought, in my yesternight's evening walk, warmed me to a pitch of enthusiasm on the theme of Liberty and Independance [*sic*], which I threw into a kind of Scots Ode, fitted to the Air, that one might suppose to be the gallant ROYAL SCOT's address to his heroic followers on that eventful morning.'

Later he continues, 'Clarke's set of the tune, with his bass, you will find in the Museum; though I am afraid that the air is not what will entitle it to a place in your elegant selection.' His fears that Thomson would not hold the tune in high opinion proved to be well-founded. The latter inserted the song set to quite a different tune, a 'soft' air, 'Lewie Gordon', which necessitated the lengthening of every fourth line:

> Scots, wha hae wi' Wallace bled,
> Scots, wham Bruce has aften led;
> Welcome to your gory bed,
>   Or to glorious victorie.

Burns agreed to this change of tune not at all willingly ('It will not in the least hurt me, tho' you leave the song out altogether, and adhere to your first idea of using Logan's verses') but public opinion, aided by performances of the song in its original form by a number of the leading singers of the day, forced Thomson to change his mind and, in 1802, he published the song as written, set it to the tune 'Hey tutti taitie' for which it was made and, for good measure, added Lady Nairne's 'The land o the leal' and a Jacobite song, 'Weel may we a' be', all to be sung to the same air.

To it all he added a handsome apology which is not without interest and worth quoting as it illustrates two of the important features of Thomson's collection; the use of English words alongside the Scots whenever possible (he usually gives alternative poems by writers such as Peter Pindar and Alexander Boswell, 'suitable English verses in addition to each of the

songs as written in the Scotish [*sic*] dialect') and full-scale pianoforte accompaniments with introductory and concluding symphonies by musicians of note, chiefly Haydn and Beethoven. He writes, 'The Poet originally intended this for the air just mentioned; but, on a suggestion from the Editor of this Work, who then thought "Lewie Gordon" a fitter tune for the words, they were united together and published in the preceding volume. The Editor, however, having since examined the air "Hey tutti taitie" with more particular attention, frankly owns that he has changed his opinion, and that he thinks it much better adapted for giving energy to the Poetry than the air of "Lewie Gordon". He therefore sent it to Haydn, who has entered into the spirit of it with a felicity peculiar to himself: his inimitable Symphonies and Accompaniments render it completely martial and highly characteristic of the heroic verses. It is worthy of remark, that this appears to be the oldest Scottish Air concerning which anything like evidence is to be found. By changing *wha* into *who, hae* into *have, wham* into *whom, aften* into *often,* and *sae* into *so,* the following Song will be English; and by substituting *Gallia* for *Edward,* and *Britain* for *Scotland* it will be adapted to the present time.' 'The land o the leal' he directs to be sung 'in a soft and plaintive manner' with the drum-roll in the piano accompaniment omitted.

One must have a certain amount of sympathy with Thomson in his first approach to 'Hey tutti taitie'. In itself it is by no means a great tune, but Burns, with his unfailing instinct for the essential quality of a melody and his unique ability to express that quality in the words he writes for it, transforms it and makes it an essential part of one of our greatest songs. The stanza with its binding rhyme fits the shape and form of the tune exactly; the words flow along with the tune and their meaning is absolutely clear on a first hearing; the mood of the words is in complete accord with that of the tune, or, as Burns himself would have put it, they are 'in fine unison' with each other.

As frequently happens with Scots melodies of a markedly dancelike character, 'Hey tutti taitie' was also played quietly and slowly, and it is so that Lady Nairne sets it in 'The land o the leal', another truly Scottish song of great worth.

One song more and I have done—Auld Lang Syne.—The air
is but mediocre; but the following song, the old song of the
olden times & which has never been in print, nor even in manuscript, untill I took it down from an old man's singing; is
enough to recommend any air.

AULD LANG SYNE

Should auld acquaintance be forgot,
    And never brought to mind?
Should auld acquaintance be forgot,
    And days o auld lang syne?

Chorus

    For auld lang syne, my Dear,
      For auld lang syne,
    We'll tak a cup o kindness yet,
      For auld lang syne.

We twa hae run about the braes,
    And pu'd the gowans fine;
But we've wander'd mony a weary foot,
    Syn auld lang syne.

For auld lang &c.

We twa hae paidlet i' the burn,
    Frae morning sun till dine:
But seas between us braid hae roar'd
    Sin auld lang syne.

For auld lang syne &c.

And there's a hand, my trusty fiere,
    And gie's a hand o thine;
And we'll tak a right gude-willie waught,
    For auld lang syne.

For auld &c.

And surely ye'll be your pint-stowp,
    And surely I'll be mine;
And we'll tak a cup o kindness yet,
    For auld lang syne.

For auld &c.